Multinationals' training practices
and development

Multinationals' training practices and development

International Labour Office   Geneva

ISBN 92-2-102569-1

First published 1981

X50786472 |8101

331·2592

-2. MAY 1981

Printed in Switzerland

TABLE OF CONTENTS

PREFACE

The present study is the outcome of a research project undertaken within the 1978-79 Programme and Budget by the ILO's Multinational Enterprises Programme (MULTI). It follows an earlier ILO study in the area of multinational enterprises and training[1] using new, more varied and detailed information, special enquiries and case studies; and focusing in particular on the impact of the enterprises' training practices on development. Despite the enlarged field of enquiry, it is obvious that the findings of the present study cannot claim to be representative of all the situations that may be found in multinational enterprises and their host countries in the developing world. They provide, however, detailed illustrations of major aspects to be considered for the subject under study in a variety of circumstances; and the information gathered permits, therefore, a certain number of general conclusions to be drawn, which are found in the last chapter of the study.

The research project was co-ordinated by Jean-Jacques Chevron, MULTI, assisted by Paul Bailey, University of Munich, who also drafted Chapter II. Pierre Drouet, detached from ILO's Training Department (FORM) to MULTI, acted as technical focal point for the project, undertook field missions and drafted Chapter III. The International Institute for Labour Studies conducted a literature search (under the direction of Robert S. Ray) which is the basis for Chapter I. Editorial assistance was provided in the final stages by Renée Marlin, Pomona College (California).

The ILO wishes to thank the authors of the three case studies: Professor Nitish R. De, Dr. Osita C. Eze; and Dr. Cláudio de Moura Castro, Sandra Ma. C. de Sá Carneiro and Ricardo Chaves de Rezende Martins. The ILO is also grateful to the Centro Interamericano de Investigación y Documentación sobre Formación Profesional (CINTERFOR) for assistance and advice; the ILO training experts and field offices participating in the survey undertaken for Chapter III; the multinational enterprises which, through the good services of the International Organisation of Employers, provided the information used in Chapter II; and officials and institutions from government, employers' and union circles providing documentation or accepting to be interviewed.

A graphic presentation of the project structure is shown in Annex I.

---

[1] ILO: <u>The impact of multinational enterprises on employment and training</u> (Geneva, 1976).

CHAPTER I

AN INTRODUCTION BASED ON AN OVER-
VIEW OF THE LITERATURE

This study, composed of research specifically undertaken or commissioned by the ILO, is an examination of the training practices of multinational enterprises (MNEs) and of the developmental effects of this training. The report provides an updated and a considerably more detailed analysis of the field of training and multinationals than was presented in an earlier ILO publication.*

This first chapter serves as an introduction to the issues found in the areas of the study. The published material is not very explicit on the relevance of such training to the broader developmental goals of the countries in which MNEs have established subsidiaries - a question which is the focus of Chapters III and IV.

Chapter II consists of concrete illustrations of the training practices of selected MNEs operating in developing countries, based on examples submitted by the parent enterprises for this purpose. The inquiry summarised in Chapter III explores actual MNE training practices in developing countries and co-operation with local institutions especially as seen by ILO training experts in the field. Chapter IV contains case studies prepared by academics on Brazil, India and Nigeria as examples of the effects of MNE training in the three developing regions of the world.

Some of the reviewed literature relates to topics not specifically concerned with training, but still containing relevant information, such as on transfer of technology, research and development, and general implications of direct investment of MNEs.

Chapter I has been organised into several sections which refer in turn to the volume of training, the type of training and the conditions which affect it (such as sector of industry), co-operation with national training efforts and government policies. Finally, the question of the relationship of this training to development is referred to, as permitted by the sources.

Volume of training by multinational enterprises

While training activities generally appear to cover all categories of staff, the largest volume of training seems to be provided for (1) skilled workers including apprentices; (2) highly specialised workers and technicians; and (3) supervisory staff (in ascending order). The number or proportion of the staff receiving training at one subsidiary of a MNE would be a valuable indicator of the training effect being made. Unfortunately, the review of the available literature has revealed only limited information of this type. Still, several examples can be found regarding that point. Siemens, for instance, reports that in 1971/72

---

*ILO: The impact of multinational enterprises on employment and training (Geneva, 1976).

training expenditures represented 4.8 per cent of its total payroll; and that since 1961/62 expenditure for training increased
annually by 15 per cent.[2] In Nigeria the training expenditures of
a sample of MNEs were slightly larger as a proportion of sales
than were the training expenditures of the national firms (0.15
per cent for the MNEs and 0.13 per cent for the national firms).
But the annual training expenditure per person trained was over
six times as high in the MNEs as in the national firms (₦231.5
versus ₦37.1 for the national enterprises). This does not however
just reflect differences in the quality of training. It is also
influenced by the location of training efforts which in MNEs are
often undertaken outside the country.[3] Thus, the Nigerian subsidiary of Shell sends over 100 workers per year to train abroad.
The company spends over ₦1 million each year on its formal training programmes.[4]

Many British enterprises have home country based activities and
training facilities for developing countries.[5] Thus, Unilever has
an international management training centre near London which
operates 50 weeks a year, with 70 managers from developing countries
attending courses annually. Metal Box trains around 100 technician
level people per annum in Britain. Lucas Industries have a number
of training centres with the equipment and staff to train people in
the skills appropriate to the needs of their subsidiaries. Since
1970 the National Coal Board of England has given training to over
100 engineers from 27 countries for periods between one week and
two years.

Some of these same British enterprises also have extensive
training programmes in developing countries, both in-house and
external, at management, supervisory and technician levels.
Training schools also exist in important developing countries.
Esso Petroleum, for instance, has had a training school in Libya
since 1962. The enterprise has carried out a "Libyanisation"
programme which required major training efforts. For this purpose
some 20 UK instructors were employed full time in Libya. In 1972
an accelerated training programme was introduced to Libyanise the
entire operation in five years.

Another example, the Caterpillar company, employs full-time
training staff at each of its overseas operations. The São Paulo,
Brazil, division has 15 people training 2,762 workers.[6] The Esso
Singapore Refinery states that in 1974-75 approximately 3 per cent
of management staff time was devoted to training activities, while
about 10 per cent of total man-days in the technician category was
spent on training and testing. In Indonesia the training programmes for the period 1971 to 1974 sponsored by Stanvac (managed
by Esso Standard Eastern Inc. for Exxon) include a grand total of
351 training courses of all kinds with 3,113 participants.[7]

In Nigeria, though, the national enterprises trained a larger
percentage of their workers than comparable MNEs: 28 per cent as
opposed to 21 per cent.[8] However, no general conclusions can be
drawn from these differences as the distribution of the percentages
of employees trained by national enterprises is skewed by a single
enterprise which trains about 39 per cent of its workers. In this
enterprise the number of management staff trained is about five
times the number of staff because of the repeated attendance of
many of these employees in a large number of short one to two-day
courses.

It must be stressed, however, that from the publications available it is notoriously difficult to generalise about the volume of training offered by MNEs and to establish comparative estimates of costs and effectiveness. Still, the volume of training carried out by MNEs in developing host countries is certainly important.

Type of training and conditions which affect it

Subdivisions of types

The type of training for different categories of employees varies and is usually designed to meet specific requirements of the enterprise. Usually in-plant courses predominate for all categories of workers. Nevertheless, many enterprises have their own training centres, either in the host or in the home country. The parent company sometimes makes a special effort to have home country courses relevant to the participants from developing regions. For example, a pilot plant set up in 1961 in Utrecht (Netherlands) by Philips Gloeilampenfabrieken, simulates many of the conditions prevailing in Africa. Workers from both European and developing countries attend. Under the intentionally limited conditions of the pilot plant, the simplified production methods as they are found overseas are used, and in seeking to solve problems connected with this approach, both staff and trainee have been forced to innovate.[9]

Another example is Shell-BP Nigeria which runs an extensive series of "in-house" training programmes at its training centres at Lagos, Warri and Port Harcourt. These programmes cover both the functional (i.e. largely technical) and non-functional (i.e. managerial-supervisory and developmental) aspects. The training programme sponsored by Stanvac (an Esso-Exxon subsidiary) in Indonesia is another illustration. The programme includes supervisory development in craft training and job-related or on-the-job training, formal education, educational assistance, management seminars or workshops and rotational assignments.[10]

The level at which people work in a MNE determines, to a large extent, the characteristics of the training which is provided. In the next section, the examination of training programmes has been undertaken on the basis of the category within which employees work, from the unskilled to the highest level of management. The special programmes can be grouped as follows:

(1) Programmes for the semi-skilled and unskilled workers usually do not go beyond introductory and safety training plus on-the-job training for the workers within the enterprise. Such training is often rudimentary and not always systematic. "It is usually not at all difficult to recruit at this level, particularly in developing countries. Many governments now levy a payroll tax, which can run from 1 to 2.5 per cent of the total payroll. These monies can often be rebated to the employer if he is careful to plan training to improve the skill and ability of his employees."[11] A special feature in developing countries is that subsidiaries may be involved in basic literacy training programmes for their workers. Thus, Philips in Brazil offers literacy courses, as does General Electric in Brazil, which in addition pays the worker half his normal wage for time spent in the classroom.[12]

(2) <u>Programmes for skilled workers</u> who have a wide range of
occupations.   This category usually gets the "lion's share" of
training budgets in multinationals, but they do not necessarily
constitute the largest volume of the training effort as measured
by the number of participants.   Often, programmes for semi- and
unskilled workers have more people involved.   The programmes for
skilled workers are usually conducted in special training workshops.
The most widespread form is apprenticeship, which normally
lasts three to four years, depending on the occupation and on the
national regulations.   Apprenticeships are usually reserved for
young people aged 15 to 18 and are supervised by the national
training authorities.   According to the information on hand,
only a few national training authorities, such as Brazil and India,
have established trainee quotas for apprentices.[13]

(3) <u>Programmes for technicians</u> such as on quality control,
work study and programming, maintenance, electronics and application
of new technologies.   Such courses are mostly internal, since they
concern specific methods and techniques used by a particular multinational.   For this category, special arrangements have been made.
For instance, Siemens-Argentina runs a centre for all Siemens
subsidiaries in Latin America where courses of three months'
duration for technicians are organised.[14]

(4) <u>Managerial programmes</u> include such activities as management
development (consisting of short internal and external courses and
seminars), industrial relations, electronic data processing (EDP),
organisation and taxation, and accounting and marketing.   Some
emphasis is also put on communication skills and frequently management staff from subsidiaries is assigned to the parent company and
vice versa for training purposes.[15]   It is at the level of middle
management and technicians that the enterprises' training activities
are most intensive.   People in these categories are often sent to
courses at the parent company for advanced training.[16]   These
categories of staff typically undergo repeated training including
study travel in a "continuous training" process to keep up to date
with new products and techniques.   For example, the staff of the
Philippine subsidiary specialising in the manufacture of trans-
mission equipment is sent to the Brazilian subsidiary of the group
for such purposes.[17]

Special attention given to training programmes for high-level
managers and technicians is easily explained by the shortage
of managerial and professional manpower in developing countries,
where rapid industrial growth is frequently combined with a historic
absence of industrial activity and inadequate training facilities.
Also, managerial and technical recruitment is sometimes difficult
because in some of the developing countries the cultural views may
be difficult to reconcile with scientific thinking.[18]   Even
university graduates often seem hostile to profit-oriented ventures
and have had little experience in business planning and problem
solving.[19]   The importance of managerial training for MNEs is
highlighted by the fact that it is sometimes conducted by an
international human resource directorate.[20]   Other studies stress
the importance of formal training both through intensive business
studies and through self-development.[21]

Furthermore, the relatively low educational and economic levels
in many developing countries limit the sources of potential talent.
The educated élite has frequently no desire to enter industry and
may prefer a career in government service.

These environmental factors influence also the selection process
for trainees.   Since the field of choice is limited, selection
is based largely on judgement.   As the companies overwhelming
need is to train inexperienced people, the major selection criteria
are aptitude and adaptability to a factory environment.   In this
process, the operating company which provides the training as well
as the trainee and the host country benefit.[22]   Low labour mobility
however, is a factor which can disturb this concordance of
benefits to the MNE, the worker, and the developing country.[23]

      When MNEs resort to subcontracting in the developing countries
another form of training is often provided in the form of help to
local businessmen in organising their production and training their
employees.   In this way, supplies are of the requisite quality and
labour skills in local industries are improved.   Unilever has,
for example, instructed firms in developing countries on the
manufacture of high-quality chemicals.[24]

      Employment market

      Multinationals often engage in activities with a high and
complex technological input.   As a consequence, they have
experimented with original training systems and methods, and they
have developed a wide range of teaching aids in order to make
training as effective and as efficient as possible.   Thus, the
information received for an ILO sectoral study on MNEs' labour
practices exemplifies the awareness of multinationals for special
high skill training which is not found in the labour market of the
developing host countries.[25]

      Many multinational enterprises pass through various stages in
attaining a multinational scale of operations.   Each of these
phases requires a different kind of training effort[26] and therefore
draws on the local labour market in a different manner.   The longer
involvement of multinational enterprises in industrialised as
compared with developing countries is related in part, to the
difference in the supply of skilled labour. MNEs invest two-thirds of
their capital in industrialised countries where high quality,
trained labour is already available.[27]   It is evident that if
MNEs wish to expand in less developed countries, they have to make
up for differences in the labour market, using a proper development
of their own training programme.   In a way, they thus "create a
labour market" corresponding to their needs.[28]

      Sectors of operation and production process

      Multinational enterprises can be found in almost all sectors of
economic activity, even though manufacturing has usually been given
the major emphasis in most of the literature reviewed.

      Selected examples illustrate some significant differences in MNEs'
over-all training contribution which depend on the economic sector
within which they operate.   With respect to an enterprise in the
chemical sector, quality control was the principal justification for
the extensive training since this task was considered essential for
the enterprise.[29]   In contrast to this emphasis on quality control
and the relatively long training periods required, the training
necessary for an electronic assembly enterprise, Motorola in the Rep.
of Korea is quite different.   A worker with at least a middle school

education can learn the scribing process for preparing plastic
wafers for integrated circuit components - a high technology
operation - in about two days.[30]   Technical training of senior
staff is carried out in the case of this enterprise through visits
to the plant by headquarters staff or personnel from other
subsidiaries;   the emphasis is on on-the-job training.

     To illustrate the relation of technology and management one
author defines the "technology gap" in terms of a "management gap"
that stifles the absorption and diffusion of appropriate technology.[31]   For the purpose of the present study, it must be
realised that the analysis of training efforts - from the perspective of a mechanism for technological transfer, which is the
angle of most of the available studies - places emphasis on intra-
company relationships rather than on the links between the host
country operation of a multinational and the local or national
development efforts.   It is obviously the latter aspect which
would be of particular interest in the context of this present
report.   Training provided by multinationals seems to be highly
influenced by the analysis of the training needs for the various
specialised operations of the production process.   Thus, in one
given enterprise training can vary in degree, complexity and
duration from the most simple level of the new worker's induction
to helping the worker complete a full university education.[32]

Co-operation with national training efforts and government policies

Co-operation

     The literature analysed indicates that management usually
understands and can provide for its own needs based on its own
perception of its growth, turnover and changing technology.   There
is less information, on the other hand, on the relationship which
exists between such an internal view of training needs and that of
the broader training needs of the developing country.   However,
these two aspects of training are clearly linked and to the extent
that multinational enterprises operate in sectors essential for
over-all development, the training they provide to their own workforce is clearly a contribution to development.   National development plans characteristically emphasise the need for the development
of higher-level skills: professionals, managers, technicians,
skilled artisans.   Thus, the contribution which MNEs can make to
the training of people in these categories - and possibly over and
above their own immediate needs - can generally be regarded as an
important development effort.   In this context co-operation with
national training authorities plays a crucial role.

     As is known from the available information, many MNEs collaborate
with local authorities on questions of training and often such
collaboration is also highly beneficial to the companies themselves.
Some of the collaboration is required by law and some is carried out
because of direct financial rewards.   But there are additional cases
where other factors also intervene, including the desire of multinationals themselves to contribute to national development.[33]
In Mexico, collaboration of Ford with the Mexican governmental
institutions has been referred to as a factor in the improvement
in the quality of agricultural production.   The agriculture
ministry provides technicians and Ford provides equipment and
counsel from its own technicians.   In the Philippines, some MNEs

have entered into agreements with the National Manpower and Youth
Council for the integration of their training programmes with those
of the Government. A general requirement exists in this connection in the Labour Code; the employer must train, for each foreign
employee, two Filipinos for a period set by the Secretary of
Labour.[34]

Co-operation between international enterprises and national
administrative and management training centres in São Paulo, Brazil,
highlights an apparent potential for closer co-operation. Interviews with representatives of 30 international enterprises in the
São Paulo region suggest that only 4 of the enterprises used the
facilities of schools of management for in-company training programmes, 7 had management personnel serving as faculty, 14 had
part-time traineeships available for students of administration and
15 of the firms had been hosts to student/professor visits.[35]
In Indonesia, the Esso-Exxon subsidiary Stanvac, makes financial
contributions to 3 universities and institutions besides awarding
20 scholarship grants without requiring the holders to work for the
company when they graduate.   Similarly, in Singapore the Esso
Refinery co-operates with universities and the Science Council in
developing curricula, and sponsors scholarships without requiring
the recipient to work for the company.   In Nigeria, Shell-BP
maintains close contact with entities in the training field in both
the public and private sectors.   This is achieved through personal
contact, assistance with surveys, exchange of training material,
provision of guest speakers, etc.   Also, Shell-BP in Nigeria
sponsors candidates for programmes mounted by the Centre for
Management Development, the Administrative Staff College, the
Institute of Management and the Institute of Personnel Management,
and assists them by providing speakers.   This is a programme of
mutual assistance as Shell-BP itself has also benefited.[36]

There are numerous other examples indicated in the literature
of close working relations between subsidiaries of multinationals
and national training institutions in developing host countries,
especially with regard to modern methods of vocational training,
the introduction of systematic apprenticeship, and in particular
improved management techniques.

The facilities of Metal Box in India are made available for the
training of students from government institutions and company
managerial staff act as tutors.   In Malaysia accelerated courses
in machinery, management and supervision and commercial training
are available through government institutes, supplemented by
specialised training within the Metal Box company.   Facilities
for on-the-job training are made available to those institutions.[37]

Staff members of Siemens-Brazil lecture at universities.
Siemens-Colombia contributes to a public fund which finances further
training abroad.   In Colombia industry gets most of its skilled
manpower by co-operating closely with the national apprenticeship
training body, the "Servicio Nacional de Aprendizaje" (SENA).   All
SENA students are sponsored by firms, including MNEs, and if the
student is an apprentice, the enterprise pays him half the country's
minimum wage while in training.   SENA apprentice training takes
three years and consists of six-month periods of formal training
alternating with equal periods of training on the job.[38]

Siemens-India provides practical training for students of engineering colleges and institutions of technology during their vacations. It also provides six months' "sandwich" training for engineering students of certain colleges.[39] The Péchiney Ugine Kuhlmann subsidiary, PUK-Ivorial (Ivory Coast), provides training assistance and delegates its training staff to sit on examination boards.[40] Philips-Brazil has concluded a training agreement with the National Industrial Training Service (SENAI). SENAI, a public entity founded in 1942, and industry complement each other by sharing the responsibilities of training industrial labour. It is important to note that the function of SENAI is not to satisfy all characteristics of specific portions of certain industrial sectors. The goal of SENAI is more general training.

Philips-Colombia also provides consulting services as well as instructors and lecturers for the National Apprenticeship Services (SENA). Philips-India provides lecturers and grants to the local training institutions. The staff of Renault-Safar (Ivory Coast) sit on examination boards and on commissions for the reform of technical education.

The inverse is also true: governments aid MNEs. The British Leyland Motors Corporation subsidiary, BLMC-Ghana, has received government assistance and Metal Box-Malaysia receives advice on the selection and training of apprentices from the manpower department of the Ministry of Labour. In India, under the Apprentices Act, Metal Box-India is required to provide training in technical and commercial trades and receives contributions towards apprentices' wages from the Government. Philips-Brazil also receives financial and technical assistance from SENAI.

One interesting programme is run by the Asian Institute of Management (AIM) in Manila, Philippines, in co-operation with MNEs. Established in 1968 by local university bodies, public authorities and national and multinational firms which finance it, this Institute provides training especially concerned with the needs of the region. AIM trains top managers who are often hired by national industry.[41]

Multinationals are involved with local training needs in many other ways. MNEs lend their expertise to a variety of other relevant projects. Transportation experts from an oil company, for example, may be on national committees which decide on the most effective materials to use for building roads. Pharmaceutical company employees may advise the local ministry of health.[42]

Despite all these examples, it is difficult to judge from the surveyed literature the total volume of co-operation afforded by the multinationals and its relevance to the specific development goals in the developing countries in question. A certain gap also exists due to the fact that little information is contained in the literature reviewed on host country governments' policies and their training institutions.

It is recognised in some of the studies, that for different reasons not all enterprises ensure close co-operation with local training efforts in developing countries.[43] Some countries, such as the Philippines, Ivory Coast and Morocco have noted that the MNEs make only a small contribution to their higher education and some others may not desire training by multinationals (thus an Argentinian law (No. 20654/1974) prohibited MNE staff, national or expatriate, from taking part in local teaching or research activities).[44]   However, generally speaking, most developing host country governments accept the presence of subsidiaries of MNEs in their countries as a normal component of their community, from which they wish to derive development benefits of various types, including a training contribution.   Certain studies have mentioned as a limiting factor for training efforts and technology transfer in general the desire of enterprises to protect market positions and their stock of technical knowledge.   A consequence in such cases may be a high concentration of expatriates in the top engineering and technical posts.[45]

Co-operation between a subsidiary and local training facilities depends in part also on the development of Research and Development (R and D) activities in the host countries.[46]   R and D units could, in developing host countries play a role in developing a local technical base and the training of skilled staff.   In many cases, multinationals seem to undertake little basic or applied research in developing countries.[47]

Basic research is usually centralised in the country of the parent company on grounds of difficulties of co-ordinating research on a decentralised basis and a felt lack of qualified and highly specialised manpower in the host countries.   In some other evaluations such centralised R and D activities increase the "brain drain" from developing host countries.   Still, examples are quoted in the literature of research and development efforts adapted to local circumstances.   For example, in the Philippines, a local vehicle assembly subsidiary produced, with the help of its own R and D work, a car designed for the Philippine market[48] and in Brazil, a pharmaceutical business is carrying on research in the country before deciding on what raw materials are required for medicines capable of curing endemic diseases.[49]   It is generally recognised that through encouragement of R and D activities in the host countries, MNEs can contribute to the growth of a workforce trained in modern technology.[50]

Government policies

Government policy as expressed in laws, decrees, plans or similar forms usually deals with the question of the training of nationals in both direct and indirect ways.   These provisions typically apply to all enterprises, including foreign enterprises. A widely used indirect training policy is a training tax on enterprises which do not engage in training or in certain types of training.   Sometimes, such training levies have the effect of promoting training by multinational enterprises.

Thus, in Tanzania, a training levy requires an employer who employs a foreigner to pay a certain percentage of the foreigner's payroll in tax.   This is clearly intended to discourage the employment of foreigners and to encourage the training of local workers to replace them.   Case studies show that the Government enforces the provisions of the Act vigorously.   The Minister of Finance has power, however, to exempt an employer of foreigners where the Minister is satisfied that the employer is making a reasonable effort to train Tanzanians.[51]   Similarly, the control of work permits for foreign workers may encourage the hiring of nationals. In Bahrain, as often elsewhere, foreign workers must have a valid work permit issued by the Ministry of Labour and Social Affairs.

The Minister may cancel a work permit if he feels that the foreigner[52]
has a position which could be filled by a Bahraini worker.   To
the extent that measures are taken by the Government to require that
foreign investors undertake the training of Bahraini workers, or
undertake the training itself, such a provision can obviously have
a direct bearing on the type and volume of training carried out by
MNEs in the country. Other nations, such as Ethiopia and Madagascar,
have similar laws providing good examples of these points.[53]

In a considerable number of cases governments of developing
countries have introduced special localisation programmes for the
training and development of local management.   Thus, as a consequence of both company policy and government regulations, a number
of Pfizer's plants in India and Pakistan have been converted
to 100 per cent local labour and management.   At times governments,
keeping their economic goals in mind, seem to require a quicker
pace of indigenisation of management than the enterprises are able
to follow.   Thus, one company in Nigeria finds that the prohibition
against hiring foreign workers hinders the company's goal of[54]
training local workers on the site.

Similarly, in Ghana the nationality of ownership legislation
(Investment Policy Decree, 1975 (329)) reserves a range of
industries for local owners only.   Thus, foreigners are excluded,
for example, from textiles, printing and publishing, tyre retreading
and the manufacture of cement blocks.   Furthermore, non-Ghanaian
shareholding is restricted to 40-60 per cent in a wide variety of
other enterprises ranging from furniture and footwear to the
manufacture of pharmaceuticals and motor vehicle assembly.
Significantly, the decree also requires enterprises affected by the
legislation to begin within six months training schemes designed
to equip their Ghanaian employees with all skills necessary for the
operation of the enterprise and for the assumption of supervisory
and managerial positions.   One possible problem of the extension of
such current legislation could be an unfavourable impact on employment of nationals in case of a shortage of indigenous skilled
labour.[55]

There is little information on developing host countries'
policies requesting MNEs to specifically contribute to the
countries' training needs through programmes conducted outside the
enterprises, e.g. at local training institutes.   Likewise, economic
and social development plans frequently set general training targets
with regard to the type and volume of skills required, but they are
usually silent about the specific contribution expected from local
or multinational enterprises.*   The need for more guidance for
multinational enterprises is recognised in a number of studies
including the need to insist on expanded training programmes.[56]

Relevance of MNE training to development

A previous attitude to development has been that training of
any kind promotes an economic development identical to that of the
Western countries, with only the time lag accounting for the
difference in level.[57]   In this view, MNEs may be instruments in
the over-all process of development just by providing access to

---

* See in this context the case studies on Brazil, India and
Nigeria in Chapter IV of this report.

modern science, education, arts and culture.[58] But there is a more
discriminating view emerging according to which the transfer of
any modern technologies and skills cannot be simply equated with a
contribution to development. Therefore, in recent years, private
foreign investment has played a substantial part in transferring
capital and skills to the developing countries. This is not necessarily the same thing as contributing to development, since the host
country and the MNE do not automatically have the same interests.[59]

Technology transfer by and training efforts of MNEs may be
looked upon as contributing to development if:

(1) they economise on the local scarce resources, and exploit local
     abundant resources, thus directly or indirectly contributing
     to economic growth;

(2) they have an impact not only on GNP, but also on the livelihood
     and employment possibilities for the people; and

(3) they form an integrated part of the host governments'
     development planning process and strategies, and do not create
     "technological enclaves" or "regional imbalances".[60]

In the sources reviewed, there is little information on the
systematic assessment of MNE training efforts according to these
criteria. In a number of studies, though, critical judgements
have been made on the basis of some of these factors. For instance,
it is sometimes asserted that because the training programmes of
MNEs are designed to fulfil their own needs, they do not necessarily
suit the over-all needs of the host country, e.g., they tend to
overtrain their workers with skills and degrees of specialisation
that are not needed elsewhere in the host countrys economy. The
question which then arises is, what would these workers do if a
reduction in the subsidiary's workforce or a plant closure becomes
necessary?[61] In contrast, it has been held in another perspective
that in some cases MNEs tend to train the nationals of the host
country only at a low level of skill which could prevent them from
entering occupations with better career prospects in the technical
or managerial field.[62] Local firms have also reported that foreign
subsidiaries poach their trained workers and the best graduates of
the training schools by offering better remuneration and fringe
benefits.[63] However, there are also other aspects involved. For
example, a subsidiary in Ghana of the United Africa Company,
distributor for Caterpillar equipment in that country, has recruited
students from two of Ghana's top technical training colleges for a
training programme designed for technicians and specialists. After
two years of training the students were sought after by government
agencies and thus had the choice between attractive government posts
and low initial appointments in the firms. It was reported that a
good many left for government jobs.[64] One has also mentioned the
importance of the "social group" as a factor of recruitment and
promotion (after the training phase).

*

*   *

This overview of more readily available literature has shown that the motivations for providing training stem primarily from within the MNE. Training initially is designed to prepare the host country personnel for work within the enterprise. Thereafter, training stresses the need to maintain skills, develop abilities to meet changing technology, provide for career development, and meet growth requirements, replacements, retirements and departures from the enterprise. Still it can be expected - as the reviewed studies tend to confirm - that much of this training constitutes a contribution to the development of the host countries. Problems that have been highlighted in this review seem to be a matter for which improved co-operation with local training institutions may provide some solutions. Another essential factor, as revealed by the literature review, is host government policies vis-à-vis multinationals. It would appear that in a good many cases the place which multinationals hold in national training efforts could still be better determined by government policies. In the following chapters some of these propositions will be further examined using original information specifically collected for the present study.

Notes

[1] Dimitri Germidis: "Recruitment and training", in Transfer of Technology by Multinational Corporations, Development Centre Studies, Vol. I (Paris, OECD, 1977), pp. 17-18.

[2] ILO: Social and labour practices of some European-based multinationals in the metal trades (Geneva, 1976), p. 36.

[3] Olukunle Iyanda and Joseph A. Bello: Employment effects of multinational enterprises in Nigeria, Multinational enterprises programme, Working Paper No. 10 (Geneva, ILO, 1979), pp. 10-11.

[4] ILO : Social and labour practices of multinational enterprises in the petroleum industry (Geneva, 1977), p. 53.

[5] Confederation of British Industry Working Group on the UN Conference on Science and Technology for Development: Training as a contribution to development: Report of a survey on the training programmes of 33 British-based international companies (1979), p. 1 ff.

[6] ILO: Social and labour practices of some US-based multinationals in the metal trades (Geneva, 1977), p. 37.

[7] ILO: Social and labour practices of MNEs in the petroleum industry, op. cit., p. 52.

[8] Iyanda and Bello, op. cit., pp. 19-20.

[9] ILO: Multinational enterprises and social policy (Geneva, 1973), p. 56.

[10] ILO: Social and labour practices of MNEs in the petroleum industry, op. cit., pp. 52-53.

[11] Robert L. Desatnick and Margo L. Bennett: Human resource management in the multinational company (Hampshire, England, Gower Press, 1977), p. 15.

[12] Theodore Geiger: The General Electric Company in Brazil, Ninth case study in an MPA series on United States business performance abroad (Washington, D.C., National Planning Association, 1961), p. 61.

[13] ILO: Social and labour practices of some European-based multinationals in the metal trades, op. cit., p. 36.

[14] ibid.

[15] ibid.

[16] Germidis: Transfer of technology ..., op. cit., p. 19.

[17] See the report by B. Villegas: "Multinational corporations and transfer of technology: The Philippine case", ibid., pp. 151-160.

[18] "Identifying and developing managers: world-wide shortages and remedies", Conference Board Record 2, June 1966, pp. 21-48; and Richard N. Farmer and Barry H. Richman: "A model for research in comparative management", California Management Review, Winter 1964, pp. 55-68, cited in Roy B. Helfgott: "Multinational corporations and manpower utilisation in developing countries", in The Journal of Developing Areas, Jan. 1973, pp. 235-246.

[19] Desatnick and Bennett, op. cit., p. 112.

[20] ibid., pp. 114 and 244.

[21] S. Prakash Sethi and Jagdish N. Sheth: Multinational business operations: Long-range planning, organisation and management (Pacific Pallisades, California, Goodyear Publishing Company, 1973), pp. 208-216; and Helfgott, op. cit., p. 241.

[22] Desatnick and Bennett, op. cit., pp. 113-117.

[23] Germidis: Transfer of technology ..., op. cit., p. 20.

[24] S. Prakash Sethi and Jagdish N. Sheth: Multinational business operations: Environmental aspects of operating abroad (Pacific Pallisades, California, Goodyear Publishing Company, 1973), pp. 168-169.

[25] ILO: Social and labour practices of some European-based multinationals in the metal trades, op. cit., p. 37; and Helfgott, op. cit., pp. 235-246, reporting on a sample study of eight manufacturing companies with new operations in developing countries, citing W. Paul Strassman: Technological Change and Economic Development (Ithaca, New York, Cornell University Press, 1968), Ch. 4-6; and Rudolph C. Blitz: "Maintenance costs and economic development", in Journal of Political Economy, Dec. 1959, pp. 560-70.

[26] Jack N. Behrman and Harvey Wallender: Transfer of manu-facturing technology within multinational enterprises (Cambridge, Massachusetts, Ballinger Publishing Company, 1976), Ch. I.

[27] Desatnick and Bennett, op. cit., p. 16.

[28] Ali A. Mazrui: "Churches and multinationals in the spread of modern education: A third world perspective", in Third World Quarterly, Jan. 1979, p. 45.

[29] Behrman and Wallender, op. cit., pp. 225-228.

[30] ibid., pp. 277-294.

[31] A.J. Oswald and S.J. Mascarenhas: "Multinational technology transfer", Management and Labour Studies, Xavier Labour Relations Institute, Dec. 1978.

[32] ILO: The impact of multinational enterprises on employment and training (Geneva, 1976), p. 29; OECD: Pilot survey on technical assistance extended by private enterprise (Paris, 1967), p. 25, cited in ILO: Multinational enterprises and social policy (Geneva, 1973), p. 56; ILO: Social and labour practices of some US-based multinationals in the metal trades (Geneva, 1977), p. 29; and Nicola Swainson: The Bata Shoe Company: Types of production and transfer of skills (Paris, UNESCO, Division for the Study of Development, 1977), pp. 6-7.

[33] See ILO: Social and labour practices of some US-based multinationals in the metal trades, op. cit., pp. 38-40.

[34] ibid., p. 40.

[35] R.S. Hillman and R.M. Moore: "Relations between inter-national corporations and management education: the case of Brazil", in Management International Review, 1972, No. 6, pp. 65-82.

[36] ILO: Social and labour practices of MNEs in the petroleum industry, op. cit., p. 56.

[37] ILO: Social and labour practices of some European-based multinationals in the metal trades, op. cit., p. 39.

[38] Business International Corporation: Solving Latin American Business Problems, 1968-69 ed. (New York, Aug. 1968), pp. 118-119.

[39] ILO: Social and labour practices of some European-based multinationals in the metal trades, op. cit., p. 39.

[40] ibid.

[41] Dimitri Germidis and T. Ohsu: Industrialisation and technical co-operation in East Asia: The case of the Philippines (IDC of Japan, Tokyo, Feb. 1975), cited in Germidis, op. cit., Vol. I, p. 20.

[42] S. Prakash Sethi and Jagdish N. Sheth: <u>Multinational business operations: Environmental aspects of operating abroad</u>, op. cit., p. 180; and Confederation of British Industry Working Group on the UN Conference on Science and Technology for Development, op. cit.

[43] Sethi and Sheth: <u>Multinational business operations: ...</u>, op. cit., p. 181.

[44] See José Maria Dagnino Pastore: "Multinational corporations and transfer of technology: The case of Argentina", in Germidis: <u>Transfer of technology ...</u>, op. cit., Vol. I, pp. 161-191.

[45] ibid., p. 24.

[46] J.D. Peno: "Multinational corporate behaviour in host country high-level manpower markets: The implication for technology transfer and foreign investment control in less-developed host countries", ibid., Vol. II, pp. 153-155.

[47] ibid., Vol. I, p. 24.

[48] See B. Villegas: "Multinational corporations and transfer of technology: The Philippine case", ibid., pp. 151-160.

[49] See Carlos de Faro Passos: "Multinational corporations and transfer of technology: The case of Brazil", ibid., pp. 192-218.

[50] Sethi and Sheth: <u>Multinational business operations: ...</u>, op. cit., p. 169.

[51] Osita C. Eze: "Multinational enterprises and local manpower in Tanzania", in <u>Journal of World Trade Law</u>, Sep.-Oct. 1977, pp. 441-461.

[52] Amiri Decree-Law No. 23 of 1976 to promulgate the Labour Law for the private sector, Ch. 2, Art. 6, cited in ILO: <u>Legislative Series</u>, No. 3, 1977.

[53] Ordinance No. 75-013/DM to promulgate a Labour Code, 17 May 1975, Title III, Ch. I, Div. I, Sec. 20, cited in ILO: <u>Legislative Series</u>, No. 6, 1976; and Labour Proclamation No. 64 of 1975, cited in ILO: <u>Legislative Series</u>, No. 2, 1976, Part II, Ch. 3, Art. 21, Subart. 1 and Art. 23.

[54] Behrman and Wallender, op. cit., pp. 226-227.

[55] David J.C. Forsyth and Robert F. Solomon: "Restrictions on foreign ownership of manufacturing industry in a less developed country: The case of Ghana", in <u>Journal of Developing Areas</u>, Apr. 1978, pp. 281-296.

[56] United Nations Centre on Transnational Corporations: Measures strengthening the negotiation capacity of governments in their relations with transnational corporations: a technical paper (New York, 1979; Sales No. E.79.II.A.6), pp. 32-33.

[57] See on this point the references in André Cartapanis, William Experton and Jean-Luc Fuguet: Transnational corporations and educational systems in developing countries: An annotated critical bibliography (Paris, UNESCO, Division for the Study of Development, 1977), p. 17.

[58] Barbara N. McLennan: The impact of transnational corporations on developing countries (Paris, UNESCO, Division for the Study of Development, 1977), pp. 10-11.

[59] UNCTAD: Financial resources for development: Private foreign investment in its relationship to development, United Nations Conference on Trade and Development, Third Session, Santiago, Chile, Apr. 1972 (Geneva, doc. TD/134, 17 Nov. 1971, mimeographed), pp. 2 and 4.

[60] R.H. Mason: The transfer of technology and the factor proportion problem: The Philippines and Mexico, UNITAR research report No. 10 (UN, 1971); "The multinational firm and cost of technology to the developing countries", in California Management Review, No. 4, 1973; Louis Turner: Multinational companies and the Third World (New York, Hill and Wang, 1973); and D. Morawetz et al: Studies in inappropriate technologies in development (Cambridge, Massachusetts, Cambridge University Press, Harvard University Centre of International Affairs, 1974); all cited in Oswald and Mascarenhas, op. cit., pp. 104-105.

[61] ILO: Multinational enterprises and social policy, op. cit., p. 58.

[62] ibid.

[63] ibid., p. 57.

[64] Business International Corporation: Prospects for business in developing Africa (New York, 1970), p. 71.

CHAPTER II

EXAMPLES OF TRAINING BY
MULTINATIONAL ENTERPRISES

Information received from parent
enterprises

     The material on which this chapter is based was submitted by
15 major multinational enterprises through the International
Organisation of Employers (IOE) in response to a special request by
the ILO.[1]   Some eight or nine of these enterprises provided very
detailed documentation (mainly in the form of internal publications
and memoranda) for the present study.   Despite these sources it is
clear that this chapter does not constitute a representative sample
of the training efforts by all MNEs (which even by modest estimates
number several thousand).   Nevertheless, given the paucity of
knowledge on the actual training practices of MNEs, as demonstrated
by the review of the literature in the previous chapter, the material
received provides a good picture of the varied types of training
offered, mainly as **seen by** management of the parent enterprise.
Moreover, the sectors of industry in which the participating enterprises are involved correspond to most of the areas in which MNEs
are active in developing countries.

     Since the method of information gathering consisted of requests
made to the parent company for data, the information obtained was
more complete regarding the **parent** company's training activities
in the home country. Naturally, various aspects of training are
decentralised and not all details may be reported to headquarters.
Nevertheless, the major features of both centralised and decentralised
training efforts seem to be reflected in the material offered by the
enterprises.

     It is interesting to note from this information that the struc-
ture of the training courses offered seem to be geared to rather
specific functions which the trainees will perform later in the
production process.   This specialised nature of the training visibly
influences both the place and the type of training involved.   The
material has, therefore, been organised along similar structural/
functional lines showing first where training is carried out, then
examples of the types of training.

Training by MNEs in the home country

     A considerable amount of training is conducted by the parent
company at headquarters.   Much of this falls clearly under the
category of management and career development and includes formal

---

     [1] A brief description (e.g. size, employees, turnover, sector
of production, etc.) of the main characteristics of the 15 MNEs
in question is contained in the annex to this chapter.

courses organised by the parent company for senior staff.   Some of
these executives in turn might also be exposed in varying degrees
to external business administration courses as headquarters feels
appropriate.   In addition, the parent enterprise also usually offers
a number of highly specialised courses in the home country or in other
subsidiaries to acquaint technicians with the newest technology.
For the purpose of training most MNEs also would seem to have either
a specific training department or a division of personnel in charge
of this task.   These do not, however, act alone.   Depending on the
subject matter, the expertise of other divisions (e.g. marketing
division) is called upon.

Senior management instruction

Examples were given by <u>Philips</u> of four types of courses organised in 1978 by the Senior Management Training Department.   These
were an International Programme for Senior Executives (IPSE) held
once a year for 24 participants (with two from developing countries
on an average) and lasting four weeks;   an International Management
Conference (IMC) held on an average of 1 1/2 times a year for approximately 3 weeks for 24 participants with an average of 10 from
developing countries;   a Management Course for Expatriate Staff
(EXPA) held once every two years with 20 participants (10 from
developing countries) attending for two weeks;   and a seminar called
"Philips in Perspective Course" (PIP) held three times a year for
one week with a total of 72 participants, 25 on the average coming
from developing countries.   For illustrative purposes the layout
of one such course, i.e. the International Management Conference,
is presented here (table 1).

Information received from <u>Unilever</u> indicates that each year
approximately 300 of their managers from overseas countries (plus
another 216 from their largest subsidiary <u>UAC International</u>) visit
Europe on work and training programmes.   The duration of the programmes vary from two weeks to three months, depending upon individual
needs.   The majority of the   participants also attend relevant
formal training courses which are organised centrally in the UK.
Senior management can attend two types of courses, those organised
centrally by Unilever and external courses.   Centrally organised
courses in the UK cover a wide variety of topics suitable for the
various needs of management of all levels and with different degrees
of promotability.   One unique feature of the Unilever courses is
that the instructors are professors of business administration
(for example, from Harvard).   Although comparatively expensive, three
such managers can be internally trained in one of these courses for
the cost of one manager trained outside the company.   A total of
26 different courses are offered per year (some only once, others
several times) lasting from one to four weeks.   The type of courses
thus offered are summarised in table 2.

Unilever expressed the view that in all the above specialised
courses a general objective was the building of understanding,
supportive, helping and trusting relationships within the enterprise.
The central training effort, however, aims at basically the corporate
managers, i.e. managers who will have responsibility at headquarters.
While the needs of all managers are important, Unilever considers
that normal management training is the task of local and national
managements.   Those nominated by national managements for selected
courses at Unilever's International Training Centre (at Four Acres,
Kingston) tend to be more senior people already exercising consider-

Table 1:   The International Management Conference
           offered by Philips

Course outline

Objectives	- To acquaint managers with current thinking within and outside the concern on the industrial and managerial process.
	- To help managers understand the role of other functions and the need for interfunctional co-operation.
	- To provide opportunities for practising skills related to tools and techniques of management.
Content	- Strategic management. - Organisation, motivation and leadership. - Management information systems. - International marketing. - Policy planning. - Management development. - Industrial economics. - Environmental subjects.
Method	- A combination of lectures, discussion and case studies.
	- A business game to exercise the economic aspects of the enterprise.
	- Pre-readings to stimulate the learning effect of the actual programme.
Participants	Middle to senior managers from subsidiaries. Age: 33-42.
Selection of participants	By the Concernstafbureau (headquarters).
Language	English.
Duration	Approximately 3 weeks (held every 18 months).
Location	Conference Centre "Groenendael", Hilvarenbeek, Netherlands.
Organisation	Senior Management Training Department of Philips.

Table 2: Unilever Central Training Courses as planned for 1979

Personnel Division

1.   International Management Seminar
2.   Management Appreciation Course
3.   General Management Course
4.   Managing Company Resources Programme
5.   Senior Business Managers' Programme
6.   Advanced Commercial Course
7.   Senior Engineering, Technical and Production Managers' Programme
8.   Senior Managers' Programme/Marketing
9.   Human Asset Management Programme
10.   Environment Awareness Seminar
11.   Organisation Development Application Workshop
12.   Organisation Development Appreciation Seminar

Edible Fats and Dairy Co-ordination

13.   Various

Detergents Co-ordination

14.   Soap Courses

Engineering Division

15.   International Engineers' Course

Marketing Division

16.   International Market Management Course
17.   Executives' Advertising Course
18.   International Marketing Programme
19.   International Industrial Marketing Programme
20.   Executives' Sales Seminar

Organisation Division

21.   Sales Support Service Course

Research Division

22.   Business Principles Course
23.   Marketing Concepts Course (jointly with Marketing Division)
24.   Research Management Seminar

UML Limited

25.   Management Course

Purchasing Department

26.   Buying Courses

able responsibility or those with high potential indicating that they will work outside of their enterprise or country.

An analysis of attendance at training and refresher courses arranged by Unilever's personnel division over the past five years showed that their management trainees from abroad were fairly evenly divided between technical, marketing and commercial training. This type of training concerns around 300 participants every year.

Another example of MNE headquarters' training is the Nestlé Product Technical Assistance Co. Ltd., (NESTEC) which offers a considerable number of courses at their International Training Centre, Rive-Reine (La Tour-de-Peilz). Courses are divided into three categories: General and Management Courses, Professional Training Courses and the "Decentralised Courses" (i.e. regional or country level courses described more fully later in this chapter).

The General and Management Courses are open to all personnel, irrespective of the stage reached in their individual careers and encompass four basic spheres of training needs: personal efficiency, business and its environment, human resources and management. Each course subject is further subdivided into specific learning segments (e.g. rapid reading, EDP for users, staff information, decision-making), the mastering of which will make job performance easier and more efficient.

The second type of courses offered by NESTEC, the Professional Training Courses, are intended for people holding similar functions within the company with the goal of maintaining and developing professional knowledge in the light of job requirements and technical evolution. Subjects covered include auditing, management accounting cash management, manufacture and control of refrigerated foods, milk powder, secretarial work, etc. A total of 27 courses were offered in 1979 lasting from 3 days to 3 weeks, mainly in English, but also in French and occasionally in German.

Advanced technical training

Training at headquarters by the MNEs under review does not only involve management training. In some enterprises (depending on the sector) it encompasses highly specialised technical training in all of their product divisions. This is the case, to take one example, for the Philips International Telecommunications Training Centre (PITTC) (in Hilversum, The Netherlands) which trained 3,220 persons from 109 different countries between 1962 and 1978 for a total of 36,684 working weeks; 1,385 of these were participants from developing countries (449 with fellowships) receiving 23,550 weeks of training. In the developing countries themselves PITTC conducted 16,030 weeks of training for 1,155 employees between 1962 and 1978.

In another case the Compagnie Française des Pétroles (CFP) which conducts professional training in Algeria, Iraq, Martinique, the Ivory Coast and Mozambique reported, as an example, that already during the construction phase of a refinery in Cameroon, an interview team from France selected 42 future host country operators for a two-year training period at three refineries of the Group in France. During the first year a course alternating practical and theoretical work adapted to their needs was followed, with the group being trained and supervised by the same experienced technicians who had selected them. In the second year they assumed actual positions with respon-

sibilities in the French refineries.   When the refinery is opened
in 1980, 31 French technicians and trainers will also return with
the Cameroonian trainees to help assure the smooth running of the
operation and allowing the Cameroonians progressively to assume more
responsible functions.   It is expected that most of the technicians
will have returned to France within three years leaving the Cameroonians in control.

        Another interesting feature of training by <u>Philips</u> is its pilot
plant which was set up in 1961 to obtain information on the problems
of starting and supporting industrial activities in the developing
countries.[1]   Through this experiment Philips intends to learn how
expertise can be adequately transferred to developing countries.
The specific task of the plant is to obtain, via simulation techniques,
concrete knowledge on appropriate technology transfer to developing
countries through "simplification" and "scaling-down" of the companies
international transfer of industrial know-how; and on the training
requirements that go with this transfer.   The autonomy of the pilot
plant (located 90 kilometres from headquarters) is thought to be
helpful.   In 1978, seventeen people from developing countries received training at the plant for a period longer than a week.   The
pilot plant has, to date, assisted manufacturing activities in about
20 developing countries.

        Group training facilities and courses are provided by the
<u>Royal Dutch/Shell</u> group of companies in the Netherlands and London
for the use of both operating and service companies.   In the main
these are courses of an advanced or specialised nature which are more
practical to run centrally.   The technical courses such as drilling
technology or refinery instrumentation are of a nature which can be
only provided in an organisation possessing expertise in these fields.

        An idea of the world-wide interest in these courses can be gained
from table 3.   This shows the breakdown of nationalities of staff
attending exploration, production and manufacturing technical courses
which are run in The Hague.   It is only an illustration since it
does not take account of the many trainees who attend courses in
other technical subjects such as equipment knowledge and maintenance
and in non-technical subjects.

Attachment/secondment programmes

        Secondment of individual trainees from overseas to headquarters
seems to be fairly common in the enterprises under review.   The
<u>Wiggins Teap Group</u> (the paper division of BAT Industries), reported
for instance, that attachment of overseas nationals to operating
companies in the UK for specific functional training was part of their
endeavours.   For example, a Brazilian graduate engineer with potential
for the post of development engineer was attached in 1979 to the
Development Engineering Department of their Dartford Mill.   A similar
attachment of a graduate chemist to a mill technical department was
planned for 1980.

---

[1] Reference has already been made to this fact in the literature
review of Chapter I in this present study.

Table 3: Royal Dutch/Shell Group Training Technical Courses:
Exploration, production, manufacturing.

Nationalities participating during 1979 other than British and Dutch

Europe	No.	Africa	No.	Middle East	No.	East Asia and Australasia	No.	N. and S. America and Caribbean	No.
Austria	8	Algeria	1	Egypt	6	Australia	64	Argentina	3
Belgium	14	Gabon	2	Iran	1	Brunei	15	Brazil	5
Cyprus	8	Ghana	2	Jordan	5	India	9	Canada	6
Czechoslovakia	1	Kenya	6	Lebanon	4	Indonesia	7	Chile	1
Denmark	16	Nigeria	102	Oman	9	Japan	9	Colombia	1
Finland	2	South Africa	7	Qatar	3	Malaysia	50	Dominican Republic	2
France	80	Sudan	2	Turkey	10	New Zealand	9	USA	13
F.R. of Germany	98			United Arab Emirates	1	Pakistan	2	Venezuela	70
Greece	1					Philippines	10		
Ireland	7			Yemen	1	Singapore	42		
Italy	6					Sri Lanka	1		
Norway	44					Thailand	16		
Portugal	4								
Spain	7								
Sweden	11								
Switzerland	30								
TOTALS	337		122		40		234		101

Dunlop indicated that secondment and full-time on-the-job training could only take place at the moment at the managerial level. The duration of the secondment for such training was generally six months. The enterprise indicated that sometimes there was resistance to on-the-job training at lower levels conducted at headquarters.

UAC International reported that overseas training was undertaken both for specific technical skills and formal courses in general management which were required at a higher level than could be obtained locally. Here attachment plans were particularly tailored to meet individual needs and programmes arranged in Europe, the United States, the Philippines and Australia. By way of example, a typical programme for a visitor from Nigeria might include two days at headquarters in London, followed by a one-month attachment to the Audit Department of Unilever's German subsidiary in Hamburg and a one-week visit to the Austrian subsidiary in Vienna. After this, two weeks would be spent in London working at headquarters' Audit Department. Next a one-week and a two-week Unilever management course would be attended before a concluding round of interviews. In 1979, 169 such programmes were arranged.

External business administration courses

This type of management development is offered by various enterprises for selected senior staff. Above and beyond their regular training programme Alusuisse finances, for instance, complete university degree courses for their more senior employees and managers. The enterprise provides this opportunity for executives from Africa, Australia and Latin America. Thus a Nigerian manager was able to finish his studies at a Canadian University and a geologist from Sierra Leone did the same in Basel. He then became the head geologist at an Alusuisse bauxite mine in his home country. For the senior external courses, Unilever also provides its staff with course descriptions and other relevant data on 10 UK universities, 9 continental Europe institutes and 15 American universities. In 1978, 54 managers attended these external courses (with another 63 doing language tuition only). Since external courses of this kind are very expensive only people moving into very senior jobs get the opportunity. Nearly all the heads of Unilever's business in developing countries have attended such a course once at an appropriate time in their career. Since the bulk of Unilever's business is in the industrialised countries, only 210 out of their total of 1,913 senior managers, i.e. 10 per cent, come from developing countries. To put it in overall terms, this figure of 210 is 1 per cent of their grand global total of management which is 21,575.

Mobil Oil Française also reported that in addition to shorter seminars for sales or technology training and individual programmes to upgrade skills (all of which could be held within the enterprise in France), the services of external institutes including those of the ILO's International Centre for Advanced Technical and Vocational Training (Turin) were engaged for courses of a longer nature.

Other education

The Philips International Institute (PII) annually offers technical diploma courses to 30 students per year (25 thereof from developing countries). Established in 1957, PII awards a diploma

to those who make satisfactory progress in their study programme
(which can be individually drawn up).   A certificate is awarded to
those with shorter periods of study (describing in some detail the
work done).   Furthermore, a 17-month course leading to the degree
of Master of Electronic Engineering is also offered, together with
a diploma in Electronic Design Engineering (EDE).   The students
are not Philips' employees and are prohibited from joining Philips
in the Netherlands (although they may join national Philips'
organisations elsewhere, especially in their home countries, as many
have done).   Scholarships are available either directly from Philips
or the Netherlands Government.   The direct economic advantage to the
company is not a criteria for these other types of courses supported
by MNEs.   Thus, to take another example, Alusuisse trained a medical
student from Sierra Leone at the tropical institute in Basel.

Headquarters courses for specific regions

Ciba-Geigy and Sandoz indicate in the documents received that
the greater the homogeneity of the participants, the higher the
chances of holding successful technical training for the group.
Homogeneity is defined as first coming from one continent and having
competence in the same working language and, as a corollary,
most likely having been exposed to the same school system at home.
Second, participants should possess technical knowledge and practical
experience in the area to be studied.   This should be able to be
equated to a level recognised in Europe.   Third, those with only
theoretical experience in laboratories are not accepted. And fourth,
participants should all be approximately the same age, e.g. between
25 and 35, as was the case in a recent technical training course.
In this particular instance success with a more homogeneous group has
led the enterprises to recommend future courses at headquarters for
specific regions based on similar requirements and for other
continents.

In addition to regularly instructing its sales staff, agents
and customers on the use of its products, the "Agro Division" of
Ciba-Geigy held for the first time in 1979 a "Project Management
Workshop" for 19 participants from nine English language African
countries.   The objective of the course was to train employees from
developing countries in the technique of carrying out large marketing
projects which until now were centrally implemented by the Agro
Division.   The programme had the following features:

1.   INTRODUCTION

    1.1   The role of projects for the AC Division
    1.2   Agro Project Management

2.   BASICS OF PROJECT MANAGEMENT

    2.1   Communication, Leadership and Teamwork
    2.2   Planning Techniques
    2.3   Principles of Organisation

3.   TASKS OF PROJECT MANAGEMENT

    3.0   Marketing
    3.1   Organisation
    3.2   Personnel Management
    3.3   Finance, Planning, Control

3.4   Administration
3.5   Legal Affairs
3.6   Infrastructure
3.7   Application Services
3.8   Logistics
3.9   Technical Matters
3.10 Safety

4.   SPECIAL TOPICS (according to markets and participants)

5.   SUMMARY AND FINAL DISCUSSIONS

      Ciba-Geigy also held in November/December 1979 an initial
training course in Spanish for Latin American middle management.
The 28 participants from eight countries came together for a nine
day course supported by "Management Development" and "Regional
Services" which covered topics such as chemicals and the international
economy; Ciba-Geigy as an MNE; Ciba-Geigy in the third world and
in Latin America; problem-solving/decision-making etc. A similar
Portuguese language course of five days duration had already been
held in March, for Brazil. Unilever also reports that specific
courses depending on analysed training needs are organised by
headquarters to cater for overseas countries. An example given was
the Overseas Personnel Managers' Conference planned for London in
1980.

      In brief, training at headquarters in the enterprises reviewed
can be summarised as follows: First of all, the type of training
offered at headquarters seems to be specifically enterprise oriented.
Second, generally speaking it appears to be geared more towards
senior management or it is high level technical training or other
training of a very specialised nature (not available elsewhere in the
enterprise on a local or regional basis). Third, its purpose is
also to expose to an international environment mainly those who will
assume international responsibilities. Similarly, attendance at business administration courses provides such a milieu in addition to the
obvious practical benefits to be derived from such programmes.
Finally, those attending will already have participated usually in
national and regional courses.

      Specific courses for regions at headquarters while similar in
concept to the decentralised regional courses to be examined next,
differ somewhat from them in terms of clientele and scope.

Decentralised regional training

      Most MNEs reporting indicated that specific training needs com-
mon to more than one country were met by them on a regional basis
through courses organised and staffed by headquarters but conducted
in the region itself. These courses concentrated on the areas of
industrial, administrative and middle management training.

      Industrial training

      Regional courses of this nature have the advantage of offering
foreign travel while at the same time still being held in the
participants' continent. These courses, therefore, leave the
trainees in their "home environment" (which cannot be said for the
courses held in the USA and Europe).

Nestlé mentioned that the enterprise has developed industrial training courses for supervisors which are held every two years in Africa (separately for English and French speaking candidates). Originally simple questions of hygiene and organisation of work were covered. Recently the courses have become more detailed and sophisticated.

One of these courses, the fifth "Industrial Training Course in Africa" held in Nairobi (1979), was organised by Nestlé's International Training Centre (NESTEC, Rive-Reine) for 13 participants who were responsible for markets in five African countries (Nigeria, Ghana, Kenya, Swaziland and Tanzania). The specific subject of this eight-day course was industrial relations with emphasis on economics and business analysis, effective techniques of work, industrial relations, problem solving and decision-making.

Administrative training

Another example of a decentralised regional course organised by Nestlé's International Training Centre was a Food Specialists Course for Administrative Staff held in Kenya in November 1978 (the second regional course of this type). The course had three Swiss seminar leaders and was attended by 12 participants from four countries (Ghana, Zambia, Nigeria and Kenya). Lasting 10 days, the seminar dealt with questions related to preparing a balance sheet with an introduction to computers and the use of EDP (electronic data processing). Also covered were concepts related to the management of human relations. The course included lastly a factory visit.

The regional courses organised by NESTEC cover a variety of economic and personnel areas, especially marketing and sales (e.g. advertising, market research etc.), production (for supervisors, chief engineers), organisation, personnel, finance-control and development. In all 21 such courses were held in 1979 in Europe, Africa, Latin America and Asia in English, French, Spanish and Italian. A list of decentralised regional courses (planned) for 1979/80 is given as table 4.

General middle management training

Likewise Philips indicated that the enterprise undertakes extensive regional training (organised by headquarters but taking place in the regions) which consists mainly of general management or inter-disciplinary courses such as marketing, automation (information systems), production management (e.g. accounting for non-accountants) and sales courses. A total of 439 people attended in 1978 such courses which were located in Colombia, Chile, Mexico, Malaysia, Venezuela, Brazil, Argentina, Peru, Turkey, Pakistan, Hong Kong, Japan, Uruguay, India and Singapore (see table 5). In 1978 "Management Development" of Ciba-Geigy (responsible for training and recruiting senior executives and managers) held a series of seminars in eight developing countries.

The regional courses conducted by Unilever seem to be more of the middle management type and are held on a regular basis (e.g. sales training in West Africa, marketing in Thailand and Argentina, advertising in Manila and Brazil, market research in the Philippines and Argentina and engineering in Indonesia and Kenya). Advanced

Table 4: Decentralised regional courses organised by Nestlé (1979/80)

MARKETING AND SALES

Advertising Course for Assistant Product Managers
Milan (Italian)
8th—13th January

Seminar for Medical Delegates from English-Speaking Markets of Africa
Nairobi (English)
26th February—9th March

Seminar for Product Specialists of Latin America inc. ANA
Mexico (Spanish)
12th—30th March

Marketing Research Seminar for Product Specialists
Scandinavia (English)
June

Seminar for Marketing Specialists of Australia and New Zealand
Sydney (English)
9th—27th July

Basic Marketing Management Seminar for Assistants of Latin America
Mexico (Spanish)
17th-28th September

Seminar for Sales Managers of Latin America
Mexico (Spanish)
1st-12th October

Basic Marketing Management Seminar for Assistants of the Far East
Manila (English)
29th October—9th November

Regional Conferences on Drinks
Language, dates and places to be fixed

Sales Seminar French-Speaking Africa
Dates and place to be fixed (French)

Seminar for Salesmen/Prospectors of French-Speaking Africa
Place to be fixed (French)
December

PRODUCTION

Supervisors' Training Course (1 week)
Kenya (English)
March

Supervisors' Training Course (1 week)
Ivory Coast (French)
March

Seminar on Packaging Materials
Brazil
May—June

Standard Cost Course (2 weeks)
Bogota (Spanish)
April

Course for Chief Engineers
Vevey
February/March 1980

ORGANIZATION

Industrial Organization Seminar (1–2 weeks)
Latin America
October

Industrial Organization Seminar (1–2 weeks)
Asia
End 79/Begin 1980

PERSONNEL

Basic Course on the Personnel Function (2 weeks)
Latin America (Spanish)
May

FINANCE—CONTROL

Regional Course for Administrative Staff of French-Speaking Africa (2 weeks)
Place and dates to be fixed (French)

DEVELOPMENT

Seminar on Communication and Participative Management
English-Speaking Africa
Nairobi (English)
30th April—4th May

management courses have also been run in Australia, Sri Lanka,
Nigeria and Brazil during the last 18 months (1978/79) and one is
also scheduled for South Africa.   Unilever also holds German,
Italian and Scandinavian managers' courses (which can be taught in
English or the local language to allow participants to discuss in
their mother tongue) and International Management Seminars (IMS) in
French (in Lesigny).

Regional training centres in developing countries

Some of the reporting enterprises indicate that they have created
permanent regional training centres.   Thus Nestlé has set up a local
professional training centre INDEC in Mexico where training for Nestlé
affiliated personnel in Latin America is also provided.   In 1978,
35 seminars were held.   In one instance 884 people attended.
Between 1963 and 1973 some 3000 persons from domestic Mexican enterprises and from other Latin American countries have also attended
courses here.   Unilever also conducts African marketing, sales,
and an advanced management course on an alternating basis for developing countries in Africa at the Nigerian UAC Centre, of its subsidiary
UAC International.

The examples provided are too few, however, to permit any conclusions to be drawn as to whether the creation of regional training
centres is a feature common to the training programmes of most major
MNEs.   One might hypothesize that length of involvement in a region,
size of markets, potential return etc., would be factors affecting
the decision to establish a regional centre with a programme run
independently from that of headquarters.   Such centres also instruct
the full range of subjects, including senior management topics, as
required for the region.

Trends in regional training

Regional training then is seen to be rather mixed although
tending to focus on what one might term the needs of middle management.   It can be conducted at headquarters or in the regions themselves.   Although a consistent pattern could not be detected, for
some MNEs the novelty of the topic, the one-time requirement of a
course to satisfy a need, or the backup material necessary for
instruction, could be arguments of convenience favouring location of
a regional course at headquarters.   For others, recurring requirements which necessitated that a specific topic be dealt with on a
regular basis seemed to point towards decentralised regional courses.
These courses were obviously not economical at the local level (where
perhaps only one potential trainee per country existed) and attendance
at them seemed to signify attainment of a certain career stage which
called for the reward of travel to attend a course within the region.
In these courses, exposure to a more international environment was
not necessary since the homogeneity of the group was stressed (as it
was also for regional courses at headquarters) and the specific requirement of the course might only be familiarisation with a regional
market.   Although some MNEs seem to have set up regional training
centres (generally locally staffed), this did not seem to be so in
the majority of cases.

In one MNE at least, the tendency was towards an increase of
the number and scope of regional courses within the past five years
so as to confer more responsibility on local staff with regard to
taking decisions regarding local and regional markets.   Another
factor connected with regional training is that of language with
emphasis on holding courses in the language of the region.   Finally,
the decision to hold a decentralised regional course might simply be

Table 5: Survey of Training Activities under Supervision of
Philips' Training Department for Developing Countries 1978

Course Organised by	Title	Aim	No. and Location	No. of Participants	Coming From
The Marketing Training Group	Professional Selling Skills	Improvement of selling skills of local salesmen	1 course in Colombia	12	3 countries
	Marketing Aspects	Introduction to the overall concept of marketing	1 course in Chile	32	Chile
	Marketing I	General marketing education providing an understanding of good basic marketing principles and practices	1 course in Mexico 1 course in Chile 1 course in Colombia 1 course in Malaysia	15 17 14 29	Mexico 2 countries 3 countries 11 countries
	Marketing II	Improvement of understanding of marketing principles in the Philips multi-national context	1 course in Venezuela	21	8 countries
The Training Group Planning	Management of Goods Flow	Introduction to basic concept of materials management for local planning managers	1 course in Brazil 1 course in Argentina 1 course in Peru 1 course in Mexico	12 5 12 15	Brazil Argentina 4 countries Mexico
The Training Group Information Systems	Basic Course in Information and Automation	An orientation on the principles of information systems	1 course in Turkey 1 course in Pakistan 1 course in Hong Kong 1 course in Japan		Turkey Pakistan Hong Kong Japan
	Project Team Automation Course	To support non-specialists, as there are factory, sales materials management, planning and administration managers, with knowledge of information systems	1 course in Malaysia 1 course in Uruguay	20 20	Malaysia Malaysia
	Managers Automation Course	To help local managers to formulate their automation policy	1 course in India	20	India
The Training Group Mental Skills	Kepner Tregoe Genco Workshop	To improve problem solving skills of local managers in sales and production departments	3 courses in Singapore	70	13 countries

one of costs; it is less expensive to bring three instructors from
Europe to a developing country than to bring 20 or more course
participants to Europe.

Training in individual host countries

All 15 MNEs which submitted information indicated that a considerable amount of technical training was undertaken at the local
level, either by the subsidiary or in co-operation with local external
institutes.[1] Most of these training activities were carried out by
the subsidiaries with a great deal of autonomy. For example, Nestlé
reported that training, like all personnel questions (including
conditions of employment, administration and relations with the trade
unions) was one of the areas considered to be most "decentralised".
The organisation of training in a specific host country is the primary
responsibility of the subsidiary, which of course can rely on the
international training centre of headquarters for support in the
organisation of courses (method, programmes, administration) and the
advice of experts for arranging individual traineeships abroad.

Acquisition of basic educational skills

Depending on the local circumstances found in a host country
some MNEs referred to the necessity of what can almost be termed a
pre-training effort, i.e. the need to include literacy and numeracy
training on the agenda of local workers. Unilever noted that a
basic task was frequently to provide training facilities for workers
with no or little formal education to enable them to read, write and
undertake simple arithmetic necessary for skilled or semi-skilled
operations and normal career development. Unilever felt that the
process of basic education and skills training needed to be comple-
mented by the development of social skills and the capacity to work
in groups and exercise leadership. In the enterprises judgement,
liaison committees, involving unions, social or ethnic groups can
play an important part in both learning about and experiencing responsibility and the concept of mutual support and co-operation

In a similar manner Mobil Oil Française reported the existence
of a basic skill acquisition phase in its training programme.
Initial involvement in a country (1958-1962) included for this
enterprise the teaching of reading and writing (Mauritania, Mali,
Niger, Chad, Central Africa, Gabon) organised in evening classes in
co-operation with local authorities. The initial stage of training
in other countries included the perfecting of basic commercial skills
such as sales and storage techniques and simple administrative and
accounting procedures.

Technical training by the local subsidiary

Due to the decentralised approach, most MNEs reported that
exact statistics on the volume of this local training were usually
not readily available at headquarters. Unilever did indicate,
however, that with the exception of very small subsidiaries, all of
its overseas operations had a manager responsible for management
development and training which in large countries (i.e. Brazil) could
be quite an extensive department with a budget approaching 5 per

---

[1] This question is taken up again in Chapter III of the present
study from the perspective of the subsidiary and host country.

cent of the company payroll. <u>Ciba-Geigy</u> indicated that its larger subsidiaries offered various training courses, on a regular basis, independent of the parent company. By way of example, their programme for Mexico included 38 courses conducted in Spanish in areas such as interpersonal relations, role playing, and courses for secretaries.

<u>Imperial Chemical Industries</u> (ICI) which reported mainly on this point mentioned making extensive use of local institutions and <u>Alusuisse</u> indicated that local employees identified for eventually assuming positions of responsibility in the company (accountants, sales managers, etc.) were sent during office hours and at company expense to local colleges and universities.

<u>Wild Heerbrugg</u> mentions several factors which speak in favour of training by the local subsidiary. First, more staff can be trained and thus over the years a core of trained people exist. Second, training by the individual subsidiary is less costly and can be more specific. Third, depending on the level of training to be reached, satisfactory goals can be achieved by on-the-job training in the developing country in question instead of more formal training which has been the main type of training offered abroad. Wild and other companies have also mentioned additional factors such as delays in the issuance of work permits and permissions of stay as a problem to be kept in mind with regard to the choice between local training by the subsidiary, or training in Europe. Lastly, training abroad takes place in a foreign environment, with a different climate, diet, style of life and social structure which can have a negative impact on the performance of certain categories of trainees, especially those receiving vocational training.

Reintegration upon return home may also be a problem, especially if equipment did not exist to permit the application of the newly acquired knowledge. In like manner, <u>Unilever</u> pointed out that the training of indigenous staff was only really valid if staff planning utilisation was undertaken. There was little value in training if the use of the trainees after training was not planned. The more responsible jobs must be available for the better trained staff. <u>Wild Heerbrugg</u> also pointed out that initial training in the local subsidiary allowed management to judge if the increased costs of subsequent training abroad would bring advantages. Similarly, <u>Philips</u> felt that "general industrial know-how" could best be transferred by training people on the spot.

Customer training (product user)

Some enterprises mention that in developing countries training can not be limited to the employees of the MNE only. Thus, <u>Ciba-Geigy</u> provides training also to those who use its fertilisers and pesticides. No further indications, however, are given of the volume and specific nature of this type of training, although the documentation clearly shows that customers, etc. frequently attend all levels of courses offered by MNEs.

Training officers

All MNEs indicated the existence of specialised training officers as being essential to their efforts. <u>Nestlé</u> reported that in one case their decision to use skilled production workers and fully-

trained mechanics as specialised training officers (detached for
training duties for two or three years before reverting to line jobs)
was crucial since this departure from their standard operating procedures meant that in this way the future generation of senior men
in industrial operations would in most cases have had experience in
training and understand better the difficulties facing those newly
recruited into the operations of an MNE in countries where these are
still a novelty.

Another enterprise the Wiggins Teap Group (of BAT) described
the increasing attachment of home country expatriates for one-two
year periods at technician or junior management level for the training of local staff, e.g. currently envelope machine adjusters in
Nigeria, development engineer and project engineer in Brazil, etc.
Unilever felt though that host countries were sometimes unwilling to
issue a sufficient number of work permits to employ the number of
expatriate trainers necessary. In some cases expatriate staff could
not be spared for training since they had management duties.

Although Wild Heerbrugg mentioned that those doing the training
at local levels should optimumly have been previously on a training
course abroad, and the apprenticeship systems employed by some other
Swiss MNEs such as Nestlé and Alusuisse imply that local - as
opposed to expatriate - training officers are involved, there
would still appear to be considerable room here for further expansion
and acceleration of this practice (despite the declared objective of
most MNEs that todays' trainees will become the trainers of tomorrow).
Shell notes that an exception to the general trend in their group
towards the sharp decline of expatriate staff has been the number of
expatriate full-time trainers working in vocational schools and
training centres in developing countries (see table 6).

Table 6: Royal Dutch/Shell expatriate training
staff in developing countries

Region	No. of expatriate staff	
	1969	1979
Middle East	10	17
East Asia	8	19
Africa	16	5
South and Central America and Caribbean	3	6
Total	37	47

Thus it would appear (based on the examples provided) that
training by the local subsidiary in the host country tends to concentrate more on basic education and vocational training. Subsidiaries
are apparently completely independent in this matter with only general
guidance or support, if required, provided by the parent enterprise. The training conducted would seem to be largely conditioned

by the labour market and the needs of the local subsidiary. It is
mainly the "on-the-job" type of training. Therefore, it does not
involve longer curricula and, as far as can be judged, probably the
bulk of host country labour force training is conducted locally
in this manner.

Indigenisation/localisation

The terms "indigenisation" or "localisation" are synonymous with
training for many MNEs since they often measure the success of their
training endeavours in terms of the number of expatriates being
replaced by local staff. In effet there seems to be three reasons for
staff localisation. The first is a legal requirement of the local
government in question (which may be enforced through the refusal
to issue work permits to expatriates). The second is an economic one:
It is cheaper to hire local staff. And third, a sound long-term
policy of industrial co-operation necessitates giving local nationals
the opportunity to work at all levels of the enterprise.

The magnitude of localisation of staff varies between enterprises
and countries; but on the whole it is a clear and continuing trend.
As table 7 shows, between 1972 and 1977 there was a 17 per cent
increase in the number of Ciba-Geigy employees in the developing
world, or more than four times the group average. At the same time
the proportion of expatriates has been declining. This trend they
felt was a result of their effort to respond to the developing
countries' justified demand that their own nationals be employed
whenever possible.

Table 7: Persons employed by Ciba-Geigy (1972-77)

	1972	1977	increase
Group employees (total)	71 136	74 080	+ 4%
- from the developing world	11 454 (16%)	13 437 (18%)	+17%
- expatriates	250 (2.5%)	258 (1.9%)	+ 3%

Likewise, UAC International indicates that its programme to
develop indigenous management and technical skills to both cope with
expansion and to replace expatriates has led to a considerable
transfer of management skills and technology (because many of the
jobs have a high technological content). In 1962 Nigerians accounted
for only 30 per cent of the managers, but by 1976 they represented
80 per cent of the management strength of UAC Nigeria.

In 1960 100 per cent of the senior management positions in
Alucam and Socatral (subsidiaries of Péchiney Ugine Kuhlmann) in
the Cameroons were occupied by expatriates. By 1979 this percentage
had fallen to 24. Responsible for this trend are the training courses
which have been carried out since 1960, so that a core of 37 foremen
existed by 1969 from which it was possible to promote three to more
senior positions in the transition period (1969-72) towards localisation. Emphasis during this time was placed on practial training.
Between 1972-77 training activities consisted of perfecting skills,

of seminars on administration and human relations and of courses
held in France.   The training capacity was increased in 1977 with
the arrival of three officers in charge of training and continued
through 1978-79 with joint seminars on human relations, administration
and leadership, together with internal retraining courses and external
programmes at institutes such as the Ecole Nationale Supérieure
Polytechnique de Yaoundé.

A similar development was also observable for the Péchiney
Ugine Kuhlmann (PUK) subsidiary Friguia, in Guinea, as the following
two charts indicate.   This evolution in Africanisation was achieved
through internal promotions facilitated by an intensive training
programme.   In this transition towards fuller localisation, a
certain period of overlap can be observed between the departure of
the expatriates and the hiring of local staff who gradually replace
them.

Personnel trends in the PUK subsidiary in Guinea

Diagram 1

Foremen and higher supervisory grades

Diagram 2

Managers

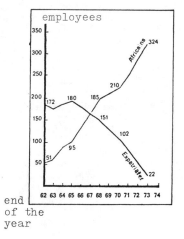

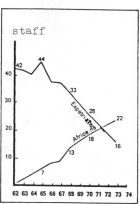

end
of the
year

end
of the
year

The Compagnie française des Pétroles has been following a policy
for a number of years, originating in the distribution and refining
sectors, which would allow local personnel to gradually replace
expatriates.   At the moment, of 9,216 employees in this sector
108 only are French (whereas expatriates had occupied all major
positions earlier).   Usually, the Director-General of the subsidiary
is local while expatriates are still employed as specialists
(administration, finance, technology).   The process of indigenisation
is, in fact, being speeded up due to improvements in training techniques and the multiplier effect together with the impossibility of
employing more expatriates in certain countries.

In some cases it was found that enterprises such as Mobil or
CFP had set up an office at headquarters or a Human Resources Development (HRD) Division in charge of localisation policies.   Better
planning in terms of forecasting staff requirements, recruitment for

priority areas, and improvement in the skills of existing staff were factors influencing successful localisation policies. One obstacle to localisation mentioned, in addition to the language barrier, was lack of knowledge by the company of the local education system which delayed the placing of local graduates in appropriate entry level positions.

While noteworthy that MNEs certainly have made efforts in the direction of the localisation of staff at all levels, there would still appear to be room for more local staff in the higher positions, since although both absolute numbers and percentages of local staff increase, a core of expatriate managers (specialists) seems to remain employed in most subsidiaries of MNEs in developing countries.

However, the Royal Dutch/Shell Group points out that it should not be thought that expatriate service is restricted to staff going from industrialised to developing countries. As part of the development of their regional staff there has been increasing use of assignments abroad and cross-postings. Whereas in the past these were mostly to Europe, inter-regional movements were now reported to be more common resulting sometimes in such untraditional transfers as between Nigeria and Sarawak, Sudan and Australia, Philippines and Brazil or Oman and Nigeria. Unilever and other enterprises indicate too that although the great majority of their managers are nationals of the countries in which their subsidiaries are situated, a conscious effort is made to see that managers understand cultures other than their own; and this policy involves recruitment of foreigners in all units of the enterprises.

Staff mobility

Inevitably in the course of a career, employees will change jobs, switching to another multinational, a domestic enterprise or a civil service post and vice versa. While mobility generally escapes notice, it can become a concern in some developing countries where well-trained staff is at a premium and necessary for localisation. In one instance where Unilever experienced a high turnover in clerical staff attracted by other enterprises, it was felt that this was mainly because these other firms did no training themselves, but found it easier and less costly over-all to recruit from companies which did, by offering a salary inducement. They recognised a solution in the more rapid internal promotion of trained staff to higher income brackets within the enterprise itself. Staff turnover can also be a measure of the indirect impact of MNEs on the level of development in a country since trained employees who switch jobs contribute to the upgrading of standards in domestic enterprises and thus to the over-all competitive business climate.

Co-operation with local institutions

Financial support/guest lecturers

The examples provided in the material submitted to the ILO show that co-operation between MNEs and local institutions can take on a variety of forms ranging from subsidies/fellowships for attendance at local training institutions (where they exist, providing that the training offered is appropriate for the purpose of the MNE), to contributing both money and manpower to bring in visiting lecturers for the establishment of new local institutions. On the other hand, there is evidence that MNEs take advantage of local training facilities for their staff.

UAC International besides its own courses, sponsored attendance at five local Nigerian Institutes, one of which, the Nigerian Institute of Management (NIM) - mentioned by other MNEs as well - also received financial and moral support (visiting lecturers) from the company. In addition, the establishment of the Institute of Chartered Accountants of Nigeria was assisted by a donation from UAC. Tuition fees of employees who pass external exams related to their employment are reimbursed.

In another case, training of local young businessmen was fostered by Dunlop Nigeria, which also contributed towards the establishment of a primary/secondary school for expatriate and Nigerian children. Dunlop India runs four schools providing education for 2,100 children of its Indian employees.

Other specific examples of fairly close co-operation with local training institutions are provided by BAT Industries. For example, the personnel director of their associate company in Nigeria, Nigerian Tobacco Company Limited, is chairman of the country's Northern Region Branch of the Industrial Training Fund and also of one of its central committees. BAT's associate company in Singapore provides instructors for the National Productivity Centre courses and BAT's subsidiary in Brazil participates financially in the cost of courses run for managers in Rio de Janeiro by the Department of the Federal University. The company there provides lecturers for some of the courses as well as participants.

At another level, Alusuisse managers are acting as guest-lecturers at a new mining academy in Boké, Guinea.

Consultancy services

Within the framework of "management contracts" Alusuisse offers complete "packages" during the construction stage and initial phases of new enterprises and projects which include topics such as: organisation, personnel planning and training, etc. While realising that the Swiss apprenticeship model cannot be fully implemented in developing countries, Alusuisse is involved with adapting it to local conditions, for example, in the aluminium industry in Algeria. Similarly, they have been asked in another study to prepare a model (for a West African country) of a complete technical school system.

Detachment schemes

Some MNEs such as Ciba-Geigy seem to follow a policy of detaching employees to serve on various local bodies which in the widest sense is a further example of co-operation between MNEs and local institutions. For example, in Mali, the MNEs agronomist has been acting as an adviser on animal production in the Government's agricultural reconstruction programme. In Ghana, a biochemist has been an instructor in plant protection at the University of Accra, while in Tanzania a physician has been teaching the control and treatment of tuberculosis at the University of Dar es Salaam. In Sulawesi, Indonesia, an agronomist has been attached to a project concerned with improving rice yields.

Other training co-operation with local
authorities not specifically firm oriented

Some of the training projects in which Swiss MNEs have involved
themselves according to information received are:

- Ifakara, Tanzania: School for medical assistants, Ciba-Geigy
  together with F. Hoffman-La Roche and Co. Ltd., Sandoz Ltd.,
  and the Swiss Tropical Institute.

- Gazankula, South Africa: Agricultural school, Ciba-Geigy
  together with other Swiss firms and the Protestant Church of
  Basel.

- Ga-Rankuwa, South Africa: Craft school, Ciba-Geigy together
  with other Swiss firms.

- Jakarta, Indonesia: School for public health service laboratory
  assistants.

In the case of Indonesia an attempt was made to remedy the
lack of laboratory technicians. For their part, the local health
ministry selected candidates (in this case pharmacists) from around
the country. Ciba-Geigy equipped the building and recruited
teachers. One of the problems faced was that lack of laboratory
instruments had fostered the habit of copying down notes and memor-
ising them rather than assimilating what was to be learned through
practice; emphasis had to be on practical work in the lab. In
the words of those teaching the course "the present idea is that
these students should go back and teach in turn". The two top
students are destined to become the successors of those presently
teaching the courses (recruited from England). Investments and
running costs for three years are borne by Ciba-Geigy. The school
was turned over to the Indonesian Government in 1974.

The Swiss chemical industry's "Big Three", Ciba-Geigy, Hoffman-
La Roche and Sandoz, have been supporting local medical training in
Ifakara, Tanzania since 1959 originally with an endowment of
Sfr. 600,000 (by 1975 the Foundation had contributed some 7 million
Swiss francs). Between 1973 and 1978, 120 graduates have completed
training at the Medical Assistants Training Centre (MATC) and if each
of them takes on the running of a centre that caters for the medical
needs and health education of 50,000 people, the total population
under their care could amount to six million (120 can now attend
the three year course at the Centre at one time). In 1978 the
Centre was turned over to the Tanzanian Government.

Problems of co-operation with local institutions

Since the existence of local training institutes is a rather
recent phenomen in some countries (set up sometimes to fulfil civil
service needs in the initial stage) it is only recently that some of
the multinationals considered co-operating with them, especially if
the multinational is new in the country. While aware of the necessity of adapting their training programmes more to local needs and
requirements, some of them, such as Mobil, still mention that it is
not always easy to know local structures and educational priorities
in order to permit an appropriate response on the part of the MNE.

In a related aspect <u>Unilever</u> felt that it is frequently
necessary to encourage enterprises willing to undertake the training
of indigenous workers by government action.   This could come, for
example, in the form of subsidies, double tax relief for companies
willing to undertake training as well as active government partner-
ship in such training by the provision of industrial training
centres.   The enterprise holds that training by the business
organisation is practically speaking more relevant for development
when it is matched by broader, state-provided educational opportunities at all levels.

Summary of findings

The above examples have shown that the scope and venue of
training courses offered by MNEs can be extremely varied.   Instruction offered by headquarters seems to be of the senior management
type focussing on career development which will not only increase
the job satisfaction of the individual but also his contribution to
central decision-making. MNEs see training not as an end in itself
just conducted for the sake of having better trained managers, but
rather for the purpose of having more efficient managers.   Such
training is carried out to meet ongoing needs of the enterprise as
a whole.

Although highly specialised technical training is conducted at
headquarters or in other subsidiaries of the enterprise in the
industrialised countries, little or no vocational training (with a
few exceptions) seems to be undertaken at this level.   And clearly
so, if the better trained workers exist then the more sophisticated
machines have to be available for them in the developing country.

Another feature of some MNE training is the organisation of
individual work programmes and visits at headquarters for selected
staff from developing countries.   Although such practices which
also include attachment and secondment respond to specific enterprise needs and the requirements of the trainee, it is clear that
by their individual nature their volume in the total training effort
is modest.

Regional courses tend to cater more to the needs of middle
management (sales, marketing, administration, accounting) and can be
conducted either at headquarters or on a decentralised basis.   Unless an MNE has been in a region for some period of time and has
opted for the establishment of a regional training centre, regional
courses provide the option of satisfying analysed needs common to
more than one country on an ad hoc basis.   They permit the MNE to
respond flexibly to regional needs;   they can alternate between
topics, language and continents as necessary.   Thus their content
can be made more relevant to the specific region.   Their clientele
(as is the case with courses offered by the local subsidiaries)
also includes customers of the MNE.   The bulk of the rest of the
training activities of MNEs would seem to be conducted by the local
subsidiary.

From the documentation provided by the MNEs covered in the
present survey, it is difficult to assess their over-all training
effects or their impact on development.   Comparable criteria on

which such an analysis could be based is generally not the focus of
the material on hand.[1]   Illustrations are given, however, of the
volume of training efforts.

In one example, Ciba-Geigy mentions spending 11 million Swiss
francs in 1976 for training purposes in developing countries alone,
excluding the costs of on-the-job training (as compared to some
7 million Swiss francs four years earlier).   Filipro Inc. of Nestlé
reported that in 1978, 2.6 per cent of the aggregate annual salary
and social charges were devoted to training.   This represented an
increase of 73 per cent over the previous year.   In another case
Ciba-Geigy and Sandoz placed the costs of a three-month training
course in Switzerland at Sfr. 22,400 per participant, or for 12
trainees Sfr. 268,000 (including flight, meals, accommodation etc.).
And as has previously been mentioned, Unilever indicated that the
budget of a training department could amount to 5 per cent of the
payroll in major developing countries.

Lastly while localisation policies appear to have been implemented by all MNEs participating in this survey, one notices that a
certain number of expatriates usually remain.   It is unclear from
the information available to what extent these are citizens of the
home country of the MNEs or other foreign nationals including those
of other developing countries.   One relevant point too, is that the
introduction of new technologies often require a temporary increase
of headquarters' staff in key positions of the local subsidiary in
a developing country.   Progress with localisation depends also on
the development of appropriate training facilities both by the host
country and the MNE.

For pratically all the training efforts undertaken by MNEs
co-operation with local training institutions appears to be an
important factor for their wider impact on development.   As
evidenced by the reviewed documentation, on the whole, MNE co-
operation with local institutions seems to be developed although
not in all cases or at all levels.   Therefore, there would seem to
be a good deal of room for further co-operation in this important
area.

---

[1] The question of the impact of MNE training on development
is taken up especially by the three case studies on Nigeria,
India and Brazil in Chapter IV of this study.

PROFILE OF ENTERPRISES REFERRED TO IN CHAPTER II (data related to approx. 1978)

Name of Enterprise	Headquarters	Sector	Production in regions	No. of subsidiaries	Sales (US$ 000)	Employees total	in LDCs
Alusuisse (Swiss Aluminium)	SWITZERLAND	Aluminium, metal refining			2 785 994	36 317	
BAT Industries[1]	UK	Tobacco, retailing, paper and cosmetics.			7 750 092	153 000	
Ciba-Geigy	SWITZERLAND	Chemicals, pharma-cautials and dyes.	Europe, Asia, N+S America, Australia, Africa, Oceania	more than 100	5 029 609	75 294 ('78)	13 695 ('77)
Compagnie Française des Pétroles (CFP)	FRANCE	Holding company, oil and petroleum.	60 countries	over 200	12 509 942	43 994	
Dunlop	UK	Tyre and rubber-based products.	7 LDCs		2 895 000	100 000	
Imperial Chemical Industries (ICI)	UK	Chemicals (plastics, pharmaceuticals, synthetic fibres, petrochemicals, dyes etc.)		over 400	8 701 411	151 000	
Mobil Oil Française	FRANCE	Oil refining and distribution.			989 048	2 511	
Nestlé	SWITZERLAND	Food products, chocolate, milk.	5 continents	over 200	11 001 848	147 000	35 610 ('77)
Péchiney Ugine Kuhlmann (PUK)[2]	FRANCE	Holding company, chemicals, aluminium.	5 continents		6 130 496	95 974	
Philips	NETHERLANDS	Home electronics, telecommunications, chemicals, appliances, etc.	In 42 DCs with the following production est. (Africa 11, Asia 19, Latin America 35)	over 200	15 121 166	387 900	46 000 ('75)
Royal Dutch/Shell Group	NETHERLANDS / UK	Oil, natural gas, chemicals, metals, coal, nuclear energy		in over 100 countries	44 044 534	158 000	
Sandoz	SWITZERLAND	Dyestuffs, pharmaceuticals, chemicals etc.			2 419 641	35 168	
Unilever	UK / NETHERLANDS	Detergents, food products (margarine) etc, animal foodstuffs, toilet preparations	75 countries (5 continents)		18 893 176	318 000 (20,000 managers)	
UAC International (United Africa Company; a Unilever subsidiary)	UK	Food, beverages, transport.				72 500	
Wild Heerbrugg	SWITZERLAND	Fine mechanics, optics.	Europe and Singapore				

[1]Information on training was also provided for BAT's paper division the Wiggens Teape Group.

[2]Material was furnished on the training practices of PUK's subsidiaries Alucan and Socatral in the Cameroons and on Friguia in Guinea.

Sources: "Fortune Directory of the 500 Largest Industrial Corporations Outside the US", in Fortune, August 13, 1979 pp. 193 ff.; The Times 1000 1979-80, London 1979; Les sociétés multinationales, Paris 1975; Jane's Major Companies of Europe 1979-80, J. Love (ed.), London 1979; and information provided by the enterprises.

CHAPTER III

TRACING PRACTICES OF MULTINATIONAL
ENTERPRISES IN SELECTED DEVELOPING COUNTRIES
AND CO-OPERATION WITH LOCAL INSTITUTIONS

Framework of the inquiry: information received
from ILO technical advisers and interviews in
host countries

Introduction

While Chapter II is based on information from the multinational
enterprises themselves, this present chapter draws primarily on the
first-hand knowledge acquired by ILO vocational or management
training experts in six developing countries in Africa, Asia and
Latin America.   These experts, who responded to a questionnaire on
training practices of MNEs, are well informed about the development
of training in those countries in general, and have a good understanding of the national setting in which the subsidiaries of
multinationals operate.   It is thus possible for these experts who
were sufficiently well acquainted with local conditions to assess
the practices of MNEs by comparison with those followed by other
enterprises in the host countries and by the national training
institutions.

MNEs in developing countries are in a unique position because
of their links to the parent enterprise and to the other subsidiaries
of the group.[1] The international character of the MNEs can
potentially enrich the training programmes of the host countries.
Although national authorities have sometimes ignored the advantages
offered by MNEs, they have, more often than not, attempted to
integrate MNE and national training efforts.   Thus, MNEs can be
approached by and can assist national training authorities.

The six selected countries reflect, in varying degrees, the
wish to supplement national efforts with the training resources of
the multinationals established in their territory.   The documentation obtained from the ILO experts and, through them, from the
government institutions and from employers' and workers' organisations in the countries concerned, is analysed in this chapter under
two main headings, viz.: (1) Training practices of subsidiaries of
MNEs; and (2) Their direct contribution to the development of
training in the developing countries considered.   Both subsections
are preceded by further observations on the framework of the
inquiry as well as indications about the general training systems
of the countries in question.

It must be noted, however, that the information on which
this chapter is based is not necessarily representative of the
training structures found elsewhere in the world and should not lead
to sweeping generalisations about the great variety of circumstances
that exist.   On the other hand, the results obtained from this
survey permit common issues to be identified.

---

[1] The abbreviation MNE is used throughout this chapter to
refer both to the subsidiary, as well as the parent of a multinational enterprise, although the latter case is less frequent.

Sources of information

The research for this study uses the replies of ILO Technical Advisers to a survey on the training practices of MNEs;[1] replies from MNEs and employers' and workers organisations obtained by the ILO on the spot and through field missions[2] by ILO headquarters staff; and, finally, information supplied by national training institutions.

The wide diversity of national situations, of the responsibilities of ILO experts and of the time that the experts would be able to devote to this study made it necessary to formulate the request for information **very** flexibly, giving the objectives of the study and leaving it to the teams of experts in the field to decide on the length of the reply and the exact methods to be used for collecting the data. The replies received essentially refer to six developing countries in Africa, Latin America and Asia, namely:

Bangladesh, where a questionnaire was sent by the ILO expert team to 34 enterprises. Twenty replies were sent to ILO headquarters, along with a short note and other documentation from the responsible expert;

Costa Rica, where the expert prepared a study based on the inter-relationships existing between the Instituto Nacional de Aprendizaje (INA - National Apprenticeship Institute) and the MNEs;

Ivory Coast, where a synthesis report was prepared on discussions held with the training officials of four subsidiaries of MNEs, of the Ministry of Technical Education and of the Office for Vocational Training (ONFP);

Morocco, where a series of meetings were held with the training officials of six MNE subsidiaries, of national training institutions and of employers' and workers' organisations;

Nigeria, where the experts prepared a memorandum on management development and attached documentation on questions of Africanisation; and

Sri Lanka, where the expert on the spot supplied a considerable amount of data dealing mainly with the training of supervisors.

Review of the local training systems

Without attempting to describe in detail the national training systems of the countries referred to above, a brief review of their main training institutions and of the relationships between these institutions and local ILO activities is useful.

In Bangladesh responsibility for vocational training is shared, for the most part, between the Ministries of Manpower, Education and Industries. The Ministry of Manpower runs five training centres

---

[1] Cf. the text of the questionnaire in the Guide for Chief Technical Advisers included in the Annex to this study.

[2] Over 20 persons were interviewed, including ILO staff, in the Ivory Coast and Morocco.

for unemployed youth and is responsible for apprenticeship training.
The Ministry of Education offers two-year training programmes in
23 technical institutes and 13 technical colleges to young people
who have successfully completed eight years of schooling.   The
Ministry of Industries, in contrast, organises training courses of
sectoral interest, such as training in the textile field.
Financing for the training is from the state budget.   The share of
education and training in this budget is relatively low: about
1 per cent of the GNP for 1978-79 is used for this purpose.   The
share of training costs in the total state expenditure on education
is, on an average, barely 2.2 per cent of the 1 per cent.

There is an acute shortage of skilled manpower in the country
due to several reasons, the principal of which are:

- the large exodus of workers to the oil-producing countries of
  the Middle East, a trend expected to decline;

- the problems of appraising of present and future manpower
  needs;

- the absence of a policy for the promotion of training within
  an enterprise;

- the type of training given in the above-mentioned
  centres;   and

- the inadequate adaptation of the training given to the needs
  of the enterprises and to the aspirations of the trainees.

The ILO has been asked by the country to help develop
training programmes better adapted to Bangladesh's needs.   This is
the object of ILO technical assistance to the Institute of Business
Administration of the University of Dacca and of the assistance
given, with the help of the World Bank, in a vast restructuring
programme.   The programme is establishing a national institute
to set skill standards and award certificates, expanding training
capacity and co-ordinating means and resources through a National
Council for the Development of Skills and Training.

In Costa Rica the National Apprenticeship Institute (INA)
currently has responsibility for both the initial training and the
skill development, either in training centres or on site.   INA
must take into account the requirements of the employment market
as well as the needs and aspirations of workers.   The Institute
is financed by a levy of 1 per cent on the wages paid by private
firms in the industrial, commercial, mining and service sectors and
by public institutions.   The agricultural sector is exempt from
this tax but benefits from the services of INA.   The Government
may in addition contribute to the financing of special projects,
and INA may enter into training contracts with individual enterprises.   INA is administered by a board of directors composed of
seven knowledgeable members appointed by the Government.   INA
forms part of the integrated training policy of the Government,
a policy which includes the Ministry of Education, the Technological
Institute and the universities.

Finally, among the external sources of technical assistance
available to INA, the ILO has been particularly active since 1967,
both through teams of technical advisers and through the Centro

interamericano de investigación y documentación sobre formación
profesional (CINTERFOR: the Inter-American Centre of Investigation
and Documentation on Professional Development, Montevideo, Uruguay).
The team of ILO experts currently on the site is concentrating on
a national programme for the advancement of workers, a programme
aimed at promoting training of the underemployed, the unemployed or
those in the process of gaining employment.   The programme is
further aimed at "regionalising" training through a better balance
of training facilities in the urban and rural areas.

        In the Ivory Coast technical education and vocational training
fall under the responsibility of a single ministry which deals
exclusively with these subjects: the National Office for Vocational Training (ONFP - L'Office National de la formation
professionnelle) has direct responsibility for basic and advanced
training of skilled workers.   The ONFP also administers technical
training centres geared towards meeting the needs of industrial and
commercial firms and towards facilitating "Ivorisation" of their
personnel.   The ONFP has independent funds collected through a
2 per cent contribution from the payroll of private and public
enterprises.   The employers' association, which is represented on
the governing board of the ONFP along with the workers and the
Government, automatically reimburses three-fourths of the levy to
enterprises with training facilities.

        A stabilisation fund, again fed by 0.75 per cent of the levy on
wages, permits the continuous financing of training activities, the
cost of which exceeds the first slab of 0.75 per cent of the wages
paid by the enterprise.   This should be of assistance to small-
and medium-scale enterprises.   Finally, the remaining 0.50 per cent
covers the running costs of the Office.

        Training in the Ivory Coast is governed by the following
factors:

-   a policy of progressive "Ivorisation" which, at the present
    stage, does not exclude a strong percentage of expatriate or
    foreign personnel;[1]

-   a large number of nationals of neighbouring countries generally
    representing unskilled agricultural labour;   and

-   a majority of enterprises with their headquarters abroad -
    about three-fourths of the enterprises in the Ivory Coast have
    50 per cent, or more, foreign capital.

The ILO assisted in the creation of the ONFP and continues to assist
in the organisation's growth.

---

        [1] In many countries, especially the Ivory Coast, a distinction
is made between "expatriates" and "foreign workers".   The term
"expatriate" refers to technicians and management personnel
recruited abroad either by subsidiaries of MNEs or domestic
enterprises, for temporary employment in the country.   "Foreigners" -
Europeans or Africans - recruited locally can be, on the other hand,
employees at any level.

In <u>Morocco</u> the responsibility for training skilled workers
is divided among the Ministry of Labour and Vocational Training
and several other technical ministries. The first supervises
the Vocational Training and Work Promotion Office (OFPPT) which was
established in 1974 and is administered by a tripartite governing
council. The OFPPT Council is chaired by the Minister of Labour
and has 28 members: 14 government officials, 7 employers and
7 workers. The OFPPT training programmes, which the workers may
enrol in either before or while being employed, reflect the needs
expressed by the different economic sectors - industry, agriculture
and services - of the country. The programmes are supported by a
1 per cent vocational training tax on the payroll of enterprises,
including multinationals. The tax is collected by the National
Social Security Fund. In addition, employers can enter into
contracts with the OFPPT for running special vocational training
courses. The national and provincial budgets also contribute funds
to the cost of building training centres or to developing special
training programmes. Finally, early in 1978 the Permanent Committee on Vocational Training and Employment was created to co-
ordinate training at the national level. The Minister of Labour
and Vocational Training chairs the committee which brings representatives of the ministries together with representatives of
employers and workers. The Directorate of Vocational Training,
a part of the Ministry of Labour, provides the secretariat. The
ILO is collaborating both in the establishment of the directorate
and in the development of the OFPPT. Also, a group of employers
has taken the initiative of creating the Groupe d'études de
formateurs, directeurs et chefs du personnel (GEFDCP: Association
of Personnel and Training Managers), a group whose purpose is to
explain, make better known, and enhance the competence of its
members through better training.

In <u>Nigeria</u>[1] technical education is provided mainly by government institutions, although some vocational training is provided
by industry, either directly or through the Industrial Training
Fund (ITF). This fund, established in 1971, is intended to
encourage and promote the acquisition of skills by workers in
commerce and industry, in order to meet the needs of the economy.
More precisely, the ITF approves training programmes within or
outside the enterprise and bears up to 60 per cent of the training
costs. Furthermore, the fund finances and runs training centres
or other training facilities. Enterprises having more than 25
employees contribute 1 per cent of the annual payroll to the fund,
which also receives subsidies from the Government. A council of
23 people appointed by the Federal Ministry of Industries administers
the ITF. The members include representatives of the technical
ministries, the States, the Chamber of Commerce and Industry, the
trade unions, etc.

A separate body, the Nigerian Council for Management Development is responsible, through the Centre for Management Development
(CMD), for training managers and supervisors. CMD does not undertake training itself but rather acts as a management development
facilitator. It is responsible for devising policies and co-
ordinating activities in this field through giving advice and
evaluating on-going training. The Centre functions as a specialised
wing of the ITF and benefits as well from the assistance of ILO
experts.

---

[1] See also the case study on Nigeria in Chapter IV of this
present study.

Increasing attention is paid to non-formal education, including literacy campaigns under the auspices of such varied institutions as the universities, the state or federal technical ministries and voluntary organisations.

In Sri Lanka several technical ministries share responsibility for training. However, responsibility for formal technical education rests with the Ministry of Higher Education. Under the Ministry of Industries and Scientific Affairs are the National Institute of Business Management and the Industrial Development Board. The former undertakes training and development of managerial and supervisory personnel in the public and private sector organisations. The latter undertakes entrepreneurial training and development, particularly in the small industry sector. The Sri Lanka Institute of Development Studies, a part of the Ministry of Public Administration and Home Affairs, trains administrative personnel drawn from government departments and ministries. The Ministry of Labour is responsible for vocational training, skills development and workers' education programmes, while the apprenticeship training formerly under the Ministry of Industries and Scientific Affairs, is now attached to the Ministry of Plan Implementation, a ministry directly under the guidance of the President. In addition, the Ministry of Youth Affairs and Employment organises special training programmes for unemployed youth, and the Ministry of Rural Development organises the training of women and the unemployed in rural areas. Management and supervisory training, under the National Institute of Business Management, and vocational training and skill development, under the Ministry of Labour and the Apprenticeship Board (during its formative stage), have received and continue to receive ILO technical assistance.

Training in Sri Lanka is influenced by three important factors:

- the almost total absence of illiteracy;

- the establishment of a duty-free export production zone;

- the government policy encouraging the emigration of trained excess manpower through bilateral agreements with other countries.

In summary, three groups of countries can be distinguished according to their training systems: (1) those in which the responsibility for training lies with technical ministries and is financed by the state budget (Bangladesh and Sri Lanka); (2) those in which training activities are administered and run by tripartite councils and financed by a levy on wages (Morocco, Ivory Coast and Nigeria); and (3) Costa Rica, in which the INA is directly administered by a council appointed by the Government but financed by a tax on the payroll of enterprises.

Training practices of the subsidiaries
of MNEs in these countries

The economic policies of the countries in which the ILO technical advisers work practically treat any subsidiary of an MNE, irrespective of its financial status, as a national enterprise. Thus, the subsidiary enjoys the same economic advantages and has the same obligations as national firms. The nature of the training which MNEs offer is defined by the internal structures, the

production requirements, the management and the marketing policies
of the enterprise.   These factors, in turn, must adapt to the
legislative, economic and social structures - including training
capacity - of the host country.   The information available suggests
that certain training conditions and practices become particularly
important in these circumstances.

In the first place, there is, of course, the local administrative and legal framework governing training and employment which
has been described briefly in the previous section.   This tends
to direct the multinational, in keeping with its own characteristics,
towards one desired type of training rather than another.   Second,
the local labour market, the level of skills or the availability
of manpower oblige the MNEs to adjust their training practices
to the requirements of production, management or marketing.
One form of short-term adjustment a multinational can make is, of
course, to employ expatriate personnel and then partially to
replace them with nationals at a later stage.   Another type of
problem directly related to training is that of "brain drain" and
exodus of skilled workers.   Third, there are the training methods
adopted by the MNEs themselves.   Considering the two groups of
constraints mentioned earlier and the level of skills required,
this training can either be given locally by the subsidiary,
possibly in collaboration with the national institutions, or abroad,
at the headquarters of the MNE or at one of its other subsidiaries.

(i)   Administrative framework

Strictly from the training point of view, no particular
obligations or advantages seemed to be involved in the status of
MNEs in the countries in question.   Unlike some other developing
countries, such as Algeria, none of the countries in this study
requires, in its investment code or other regulations, that MNEs
conduct at least a certain minimum amount of training.

Similarly, there are very few instances where the status of
foreign companies or enterprises carries with it any direct advantages, with the possible exception of Costa Rica where MNEs enjoy
exemption from import duty on certain items including training
materials.

The training taxes and other compulsory contributions levied
on national enterprises are also equally applied to MNEs.
However, it should be noted that certain sectoral exemptions
applied, for example to agriculture and mining, can benefit certain
MNEs.   This kind of exemption is granted to the agricultural sector
in Costa Rica.   Although enterprises in this sector are exempt
from paying the payroll tax, they still use the training facilities
of the INA.   Because the export-oriented agricultural sector is
largely in the hands of multinational enterprises (banana plantations, coffee, etc.), the MNEs benefit most from the tax exemption.

Where financial regulations govern the use of foreign exchange
or the export of national currency, the MNEs can use their other
subsidiaries or their headquarters to train their personnel abroad
more easily than national enterprises.   The MNEs' special advantage
is particularly helpful in granting foreign exchange stipends to
fellows abroad when some of the regulations in force apparently
encourage training overseas without providing for the necessary
foreign exchange requirements.

Although the available information is not always very explicit
on the subject, the obligation to employ certain categories of
persons trained by the enterprises can result, in the Ivory Coast
for example, in these enterprises adopting a restrictive training
policy combined with strong competition with other employers
regarding employment conditions.

Finally, the absence of legislation, as in Morocco, for the
co-ordination and control of training programmes of private enterprises, can adversely affect occupational mobility and the development of the labour force.   In the first case, the absence of
proficiency certificates recognised in the labour market more or
less binds the worker to his enterprise or even to a particular
workplace.   In the second case, the absence of flexibility in the
choice of programmes or in the recognition of equivalent diplomas
and certificates leads to a waste of training efforts through a
repetition of programme contents.   In such a situation, professional mobility of a more limited kind can exist, however, for
well-trained workers who are attracted to better paying jobs by
other enterprises.

There clearly is, then, a framework, or at least a network,
of obligations and constraints peculiar to each country which guide
and modify the training practices of each MNE.   This framework
is rather vague because the plans or investment codes rarely define
the training objectives in operational terms.   MNEs enjoy as a
consequence relatively wide freedom of action in training matters.
This could perhaps lead them to frame their training policies much
in terms of their own growth objectives which are not necessarily
always compatible with the economic and social development
priorities of the host country.

(ii) <u>Training needs and conditions</u>
      <u>which affect them</u>

The growth policy of the foreign subsidiary implies varying
training needs depending on whether the enterprise is in the process
of installation, expansion or stabilisation of its operations.
The training needs are also dictated by the type of production
activities of the enterprise and by the manpower resources available
locally or outside the country.   These are problems common to all
industrial, agricultural or service enterprises in any country.
However, certain problems assume a different degree of urgency or
different forms depending on whether the firm involved is the
subsidiary of an MNE or is a national company.   Among such problems
are the level of skills required, the training implications of the
methods of recruitment, the emigration of skills and the "brain
drain", and the policies relating to the "localisation" of staff.

<u>Levels of training required</u>

The identification of training needs seems, paradoxically, to
create difficulties for many MNEs, possibly because of the lack of
trained managers or the absence of local training facilities for
specialists in this field.   MNEs therefore often seek the help of
consulting firms in preparing training estimates and plans.

In Morocco several training directors of MNE subsidiaries expressed interest in ILO assistance in this field. In the Ivory Coast the official campaign in favour of training has led many companies, and in particular MNEs, to develop training activities without any clear idea of priorities. Most MNEs do, of course, have a training structure, but the subsidiary is not always able to separate itself from the training standards of its headquarters, even when these standards are not particularly suited to local conditions because of the need for adaptation to the techniques used or the manpower available.

In the six countries examined, MNEs do not seem to face major recruitment or training problems for their specialised or skilled staff. They usually consider the quality of initial training given by national institutions inferior to the enterprises' needs (Sri Lanka, Bangladesh), but they are, however, in a position to offer complementary training to local graduates. The MNEs thus raise the level of skills to that required for the jobs.

This practice can result in specialisation which is sometimes criticised by both the local trade unions and the governments. The employers, however, base their claim on the need for job specialisation on the fact of the lower technical ability of the available domestic manpower. The survey uncovered an interesting case of difference of opinion on training policy between the parent company of an enterprise operating in the plantation field and its subsidiary. The parent company favoured a high degree of speciali- sation in training in order to ensure immediate returns on the investment in training, while the subsidiary favoured training of a more general character in order to encourage internal promotions. In this difference of opinion the alternative orientation for growth and development seems to be reflected. One might also refer here to the question raised in the course of the interviews by an official of an employers' organisation: "Can one really require an enterprise, whether multinational or not, to give multi-faceted training when it only requires its workers to perform routine and specific tasks? Should not a solution to this problem be sought through a better sharing of responsibilities between the official training institutions and the enterprises?"

One encounters another type of difficulty in countries such as Bangladesh and Sri Lanka where the Governments apply a policy of encouraging the departure of skilled manpower. The MNEs recruit the best candidates to whom they give supplementary training. These trainees are then excellent candidates for the exodus to the Middle East. For example, one enterprise in Bangladesh trains only the local welders who are able to meet international standards. As a result, 30 per cent of these trained workers emigrate each year. However, discussions with enterprise managers in the six countries being considered in this chapter indicate that shortage of technicians and foremen is a much more acute problem. Often it is a triple problem as it depends on recruitment, rate or turn- over and internal promotion.

Training of foremen is carried out primarily within the enterprise or, in any case, while the worker is employed. The training can be either on the spot or abroad. Internal promotion for these positions becomes all the more difficult when it has to be given to workers with insufficient or too narrow basic training. On the other hand, external recruitment at this level runs into opposition from the workers in the enterprise. The public

education and industrial training efforts made in countries such
as the Ivory Coast leads training officials to hope that it will
be possible to overcome step by step the shortage of local foremen
and thus reduce the number of expatriates.

The availability of technicians and middle-level managers in
a country is so important in some cases that the directors of MNEs
operating in Costa Rica do not hesitate to describe it as one of the
main factors that have led their companies to establish a subsidiary
there.   Unfortunately, the information available is not sufficient
to determine whether the importance of this factor is due to the
technologies applied in the enterprise, to the fact that it takes
longer to train technicians than skilled workers, or to the fact
that the Costa Rican pay scale is lower than that for technicians
with similar skills working in other countries.

Finally, there is the over-all problem of the training of
general management and production staff.   The advanced technologies applied by the industries call for levels of competence which
are rare in the countries under investigation.   Therefore, there
must be relatively heavy expenditures on training, particularly
if the enterprise wishes to avoid filling the posts with expatriates.
Management and supervisory training absorb a large part of the
training budget of the MNEs covered in the study, particularly
because of the perceived need to train such managers abroad.[1]
All the economic sectors surveyed were concerned about the shortage
of managerial staff, including the banana plantation sector in
Costa Rica which gives priority to training middle-level supervisors
and general management staff.

Recruitment and training facilities

MNEs in the process of setting up operations or those already
established in a country face the same recruitment problems which
confront national enterprises.   However, MNEs have a certain number
of advantages over national firms, e.g. working conditions offered by
MNEs, prestige and formal and informal training opportunities available to their staff. If the recruitment of specialised or skilled manpower apparently does not pose any major problems in the enterprises
examined, this is largely due to the training facilities or supplementary training agreements which the enterprises have.   Even where
certain enterprises in Bangladesh reported recruitment difficulties,
the analysis of the sample available did not show that the difficulties were of a sectoral nature.

The possibilities of improving recruitment through training are
large and depend on the legislation in force.   Thus, in Costa Rica
enterprises are required to take on apprentices in proportion to
the number of workers they employ and to pay the trainees 75 per
cent of the minimum wage for the first two years of apprenticeship
and 100 per cent for the third year.   It would appear, in fact,
that the majority of MNEs recruit a larger number of apprentices
than required by law and, in addition, already pay them the full
minimum wage during the first year.

---

[1] Cf. Chapter II of this report.

In Morocco, the absence of standardisation and co-ordination of training activities enables all large enterprises (not only the MNEs) to train staff without having to grant them any certificates upon completion of the course and without being required to hire all the workers they train.   Thus, they do not have to worry about the opportunities for those they do not employ.   The firms then can combine training policy with selection and reduction of staff turnover.   In contrast, in the Ivory Coast, the National Training Office, under the terms of its training contracts with enterprises, only reimburses the training costs for trainees hired by the enterprise when they have finished training.

The recruitment by MNEs of more or less illiterate manpower poses special training problems, particularly in rural areas.   In countries where the illiteracy rate is low, as in Costa Rica, the illiterate workers are employed by the plantations.   Similarly, in Sri Lanka, where 78 per cent of the population is literate, the illiterate workers are mainly manual labourers.   For these tasks a few hours of training is sufficient.   But if a large segment of the economically active population is illiterate, training should cover not only specific job skills but also skills needed to facilitate advancement.   Efforts along these lines are noted in the Ivory Coast on behalf of immigrant plantation labour from Upper Volta, but those responsible for the training frankly admit that the results have been rather disappointing due, perhaps, to the lack of interest shown by the workers concerned.

Because middle and higher-management personnel are in short supply, with gaps in their basic training and have high requirements imposed upon them by modern technology, MNEs as well as national enterprises usually compete with each other for the better qualified candidates.   Sometimes the enterprises agree on the distribution of the services of the best talents available.

Some enterprises, in Costa Rica in particular, prefer to recruit young people with good university qualifications rather than encourage promotion from the ranks, even if, as is generally the case, expensive supplementary training has to be given.   On the other hand, in Morocco and the Ivory Coast the majority of the MNEs surveyed seem to favour experienced managerial staff.   In Morocco some enterprises declare that half of their management staff has had some previous professional experience, while the other half has risen through internal promotions.   In two cases which came to the attention of the ILO experts, collective agreements stipulate that all posts should be filled, as a matter of priority, by workers of the enterprise entitled to promotion.

It was also found that several agreements exist between multi-nationals which seek either to avoid exaggerated turnover of workers from one enterprise to another, or to facilitate such transfers. Thus, for example, in one of the countries studied, the two tyre manufacturing enterprises which up to now have not been able to reach agreement on common training programmes, have nevertheless agreed not to recruit a worker leaving the other enterprise until six months have elapsed.   The Moroccan employers' organisation, on the other hand, mentions a number of agreements covering temporary or permanent detachment of supervisory staff from one enterprise to another, including the exchange of supervisory personnel.   Such agreements are not necessarily peculiar to MNEs, as one case of exchange of management staff between a large national firm and an MNE is known to have occurred.

Exodus and indigenisation of staff

It is often difficult for an enterprise to retain skilled staff who are mostly trained at great expense; it is all the more so in the case of MNEs when such personnel is scarce and coveted by other firms. Over and above this internal competition in the developing countries is the temptation to emigrate, more or less encouraged by some governments. Here again, training in the handling of the latest technologies or in keeping with international standards utilised by MNEs undoubtedly makes the multinational enterprises the principal potential victims of the exodus of skills. Two important reservations must, however, be made. First, often the better working conditions offered by MNEs are aimed at encouraging staff stability; second, one might well ask whether the MNEs themselves do not encourage the transfer of some of their staff (the more skilled) to their other subsidiaries or to head-quarters. This is a controversial question. The information relating to Costa Rica seems to suggest that the MNEs in the country do in fact encourage the departure of Costa Rican managerial staff to subsidiaries in other countries. The same appears to be the case in Sri Lanka and Bangladesh. On the contrary, in Morocco and the Ivory Coast the local subsidiaries consider the national management cadres too scarce to allow them to depart permanently to other subsidiaries in the group. Also, the Nigerian Government refused to allow redundant staff of an MNE to be transferred to another subsidiary of the group in Saudi Arabia.

At the level of skilled workers it is more a question of government policy towards the emigration of their nationals. The immediate consequence of any large-scale migration is naturally a substantial increase in training costs which the authorities and the enterprises have to bear. Therefore, it does not seem likely, at least as far as Morocco is concerned, that local MNEs encourage their skilled workers to emigrate. Such emigration occurs mainly through family connections or personal relations between émigré workers and those wishing to emigrate. An interesting aspect in this context would be the policies practised by MNEs to help their returning migrant workers to find jobs with their subsidiaries in their home countries - a question which could not be examined here. At a macro level, such emigration may alleviate unemployment.

The replacement of expatriate management staff by nationals is an objective that is common to all the countries covered by the study. The progress made in the achievement of this goal tends, however, to vary. Out of the 20 MNE subsidiaries surveyed in Bangladesh, 10 do not have any expatriate executive staff. The 10 others have an average of 2 expatriate senior staff members. The situation in Sri Lanka is rather similar: a few key posts are still filled by expatriates. In Morocco and particularly in the Ivory Coast, the character of the situation is different because of the deliberate policy towards progressive "Moroccanisation" and "Ivorisation". A strong trend in this direction is noticeable and is matched by a corresponding training effort. Thus, one enter-prise in Morocco proposes to reduce the number of expatriates employed from 13 to 2 between now and 1982. Another MNE plans to reduce the number from 5 to 1 by 1980. Interestingly, it is not only multinational enterprises that employ expatriate managers. Such persons are also employed by national public and private enter-prises. Thus, in the agricultural sector of the Ivory Coast, 12 companies entirely locally owned employ 7 expatriate managers, while the 8 wholly foreign-owned enterprises in the same sector employ 24.

As a rule, national managers are trained by serving as under-
studies of the expatriate manager whom they are to replace. Such
counterpart arrangements often lead to the doubling of jobs, with
the expatriates and the local managers sharing responsibilities.
In this case real training conducted in a specified and short time
period does not occur. Moreover, if one bears the conclusions of
a Nigerian symposium in mind that "The indigenisation programme
should be used not just to promote Nigerian businessmen but to
stimulate and push them in the direction of greater social
sensitivity and responsibility"[1] the conclusion suggests itself
that the mere doubling of jobs will not be sufficient to meet the
goal of indigenisation defined in these terms.

It is clear that the proportion of expatriates also varies
according to the length of time an MNE has been operating in a
country and the size of the MNE. During the initial phase of
establishment there is greater need for expatriate managers and
technicians, even if only to train and familiarise the local
personnel. For this reason countries which regulate the employment
of expatriates - Costa Rica, for example, where the expatriate
contingent of the staff is limited to 10 per cent - allow exception
in the first five years, and it should be pointed out too that in
actual practice the goal of 10 per cent is rarely achieved.[2]

When they have reached the stage of expansion or stabilisation
of growth, many large multinational enterprises decide it is time
to "indigenise" their staff. The upgrading of local staff through
training facilities at their disposal offers a double advantage of
being cheaper and of facilitating the company's integration into
the local scene. It frequently is sufficient to keep a very small
number of expatriates in key posts. Medium-size MNEs do not always
have the same facilities at their disposal. Moreover, their
position in international or national markets is more vulnerable
and such enterprises, in fact, show the greatest resistance to
investing in "indigenisation" programmes. Some Moroccan officials
interviewed even go to the extent of regarding internal promotions
as a disguised form of resistance to Moroccanisation because the
MNEs use the inadequate qualifications of the local executives and
technicians as a justification for the continued presence of
expatriate counterparts.

An unexpected consequence of indigenisation, at least in the
Ivory Coast and Morocco, is the greater mobility of national
managerial cadres which results in successive transition (accompanied
by corresponding training) from an MNE to a national enterprise and
then from this national enterprise to another MNE and so forth,
with each move also resulting in a promotion.

---

[1] Nigeria's Indigenisation Policy, Proceedings of the 1974
Symposium (Ibadan, Nigeria, the Nigerian Economic Society), p. 78.

[2] Cf. the examples presented in Chapter II of this study on
the experience of a variety of MNEs in various countries and regions
of the world with respect to "localisation".

(iii)   Training methods and techniques

The ILO experts in the field have commented on the relationship between training practices and the needs of the MNEs.
According to the experts, these needs appear to be dictated more
by technical considerations than by the specific characteristics
of the MNEs.   On the other hand, the satisfaction of these needs
leads the MNE to draw on three types of resources: installation
of its own training facilities; use of local facilities; and
recourse to training abroad, frequently, but not always, at its
headquarters or at other subsidiaries of the group.[1]

Own training facilities

At first the subsidiaries of MNEs in developing countries
inevitably inherit the training structures and habits of their
headquarters.   It is up to them to either develop these in keeping
with local circumstances or, alternately, to train without considering efficiency.

In all the enterprises covered by this study the internal
training function was largely fulfilled either by the administrative division or by a department specifically responsible for
training.   Moreover, the training function is regarded, in
Costa Rica for example, as an important instrument of enterprise
policy not only for the promotion of productivity but also for
the improvement of labour-management relations and for better job
adaptation.

The training methods applied by enterprises vary considerably.
The MNEs frequently draw on local or external training facilities
and supplement this with training of their own.   The training of
skilled manpower is, more often than not, in business, technical
or commercial subjects to familiarise the workers with the
equipment used.

In-plant training is the method most frequently applied.
Fifteen out of 20 firms in Bangladesh use this kind of training as
shown in table 1.

Such training is conducted either by the heads of work teams
who may have been given some preparatory training or through
trainers, detached, if necessary, from other subsidiaries or from
headquarters.   Use of the second alternative is particularly
frequent during the installation phase.   In some cases the enterprises set up their training centre even before the factory begins
its operations.   This happened, for example, in the case of an
aluminium-producing complex which started training 120 production
workers two years before operations began.

Most of the multinational enterprises surveyed state that they
have a "training centre".   However, the definition of a centre can
range from the availability of a lecture room and practical training
given in the plants to sophisticated installations under the direction of trained instructors and consisting of conference halls and
training workshop rooms.

---

[1] See the examples in Chapter II of this report.

Table 1:   Bangladesh - type of local training
           offered by MNEs

No. of workers in the enterprise	In-plant training	In govt. trg. inst.	Combined training in and outside plant	Total no. of enterprises by no. of workers
0- 25	1		1	5
26-100	5	3	1	6
101-300	4	4	2	4
301-500	4	3	2	4
over 500	1	1	1	1
	15	11	7	20

Source: Replies by ILO technical advisers.

The reasons for establishing company training centres are often complex.   There are naturally the cases where the training given is not available in the country concerned or where the quantitative needs are sufficiently large for an enterprise or a group of enterprises to set up its own centre.   It is not unusual for a company's centre to receive financial assistance from national institutions, either through a partial reimbursement of costs or through total or partial exemption from training taxes.

There are also instances where the production cycle calls for in-plant training, either for technological reasons or for reasons connected with the organisation of work.   However, in a tyre factory included in the survey, the training programmes conflicted with the need to maintain a continuous chain of production.   When workers attended training courses, they, their instructors, and the equipment they used were not available for production.   It therefore became necessary to organise training courses at the national centres that were longer and specifically adapted to the needs of the enterprise.

Quite frequently MNEs' in-plant training provides the supplementary or advanced training necessary to improve the qualifications of the workers and to bring their skills up to the level required by the technology used or by the positions they hold.   The training is provided by expatriate or national instructors or by foremen and supervisors.   In the aluminium complex previously referred to, 412 expatriate instructors were employed to train workers in 1962 when the plant was beginning production.   By 1973 the number of expatriates had dropped to 30.

Some companies try to provide individual "à la carte" training, entirely or partially within the enterprise.   Often the firm must assess the individual's need and capacity for further training and the skills required for a particular job.   This kind of highly specialised training, a type previously referred to in this report, is fairly common in the industrial and agricultural sectors of the economy.

Apprenticeship training by MNEs is very widespread in Costa Rica, Sri Lanka and Bangladesh. MNEs use apprenticeship either to fulfil legal obligations or as part of the companies' training policy. The quality of the training, however, is very uneven judged by the replies received.

Finally, literacy and skill improvement courses are often taught at the multinational enterprises outside working hours. Literacy courses are usually optional. A review of the training activities from 1966 to 1979 of one MNE, whose main product is fibro cement articles, discloses very marked trends in training needs (table 2).   In the initial stages the main emphasis is on the training of production personnel. After about 1973 the accent is on the training of middle- and higher-level supervisors. Generally speaking, company facilities for training the last-mentioned category of staff are much more limited than for the other categories. For managerial staff and higher executives the MNEs run internal seminars using audio-visual aids from the headquarters. Lecturers or discussion leaders from headquarters or other subsidiaries often direct the seminars.

Local training facilities

The training facilities available to the subsidiary of an MNE in the host country are naturally the same as those available to all other enterprises.   These include:

- the vocational training centres operated by official bodies;

- the vocational training centres operated by private organisa-tions (professional groups, religious bodies, etc.);

- the facilities offered by other enterprises;

- various courses run by universities, productivity institutes, etc. (evening classes, correspondence courses, courses run by public or semi-public bodies, etc.);

- the services of consulting firms; and

- other seminars and working groups.

Where a sufficiently effective training structure exists, relatively close co-operation normally develops between the MNEs and the national institutions.   Such collaboration is based mostly on a desire to co-ordinate efforts.   In Bangladesh, Costa Rica, the Ivory Coast and Morocco it is possible for MNEs to sign con-tracts with national institutions.   The institutions then offer courses adapted to the MNEs' needs.   In some cases the state institution may place instructors at the disposal of the enterprise. Thus, out of 42 enterprises employing more than 1,000 workers in the Ivory Coast, 29 (or 69 per cent) participated in a training programme.   The programme was organised by the ONFP, the National Vocational Training Office.   Almost all of the enterprises whose workers participated were MNE subsidiaries.

In Sri Lanka basic or initial training is provided by national bodies.   However, the recent creation of a free trade zone and official statements on the subject suggest that the Government intends to pressure the MNEs that will settle in the zone into improving the national training capacity.

Table 2: Trends in in-plant training activities of one subsidiary of an MNE in the cement pipeline sector: 1966-79

(Number of persons trained in Morocco)

Year	General knowledge, literacy	Technical training	Special technology	Safety first aid	Clerical training	Office management	Middle-level supervisors (gen. trg.)	Supervisory training
1966/67	13	4						1
67/68	15	8						1
68/69	19	8		2		6		
69/70	16	6		3			1	
70/71	9	5		2				
71/72	4	6		1		1		
72/73	2	2	2	34		2		5
73/74						1	1	5
74/75					1	1	3	
75/76						2	2	
76/77				4	3		4	15
77/78			2			2	21	
78/79	3	3	22	32	2	5	3	

Source: Data submitted for ILO inquiry.

The quality of training offered by national bodies is often inferior to the standards required by MNE subsidiaries. MNEs compensate for this deficiency through in-plant training programmes (as already mentioned, in Bangladesh 15 out of 20 enterprises surveyed act along these lines) or through under-rating the diplomas issued by national training bodies or institutes. There have thus been cases of technicians employed as skilled workers.

The national institutions often promote inter-enterprise or sectoral training programmes. The MNEs naturally benefit from this. In one country studied, for example, there is a training programme for maintenance mechanics and electricians working in the agro-food industry sector. This sector includes 32 private companies; only 2 are operated entirely with national capital.

Inter-sectoral training projects are also being developed in Morocco. There the National Office makes funds or facilities available for this type of training. Attempts to encourage direct training contacts between enterprises in Morocco have often failed. Accordingly, the National Office's new effort involves setting up a factory-school for the entire cement industry. This project should lead, in the long run, to the creation of a national research institute which should strengthen the already existing collaboration between MNEs and national enterprises in the Moroccan cement industry. In Costa Rica a continuing dialogue between the INA and individual enterprises seeks to ensure that the training courses offered are adapted to the needs of the enterprises. Thus, the banana planta- tions, which are all MNEs, have specifically requested that the INA provide training courses for middle- and upper-level personnel. As a result, most of the courses taught for these enterprises are concerned with production, planning, human relations, training, decision making or management. Moreover, the plantations often have access to the INA mobile training units.

In addition to institute and training bodies directly affiliated with or under the auspices of the ministries, the MNEs also use the services of private training bodies and consulting firms. The latter deal mainly with assessing the training needs of an enter- prise and with assisting sectoral projects. Consultants are rarely involved directly in matters of vocational training. On the other hand, their assistance is frequently sought in the organisation of seminars and more advanced training courses. It should be noted, however, that although established locally, some consulting firms work with the subsidiary on the basis of contracts signed with the MNE's headquarters.

Courses intended for personal development, such as classes in foreign languages, drafting and applied logic, are often offered externally and after working hours. Workers enrol in private or public institutions, and the enterprises refund part or all of the cost if the trainee is successful. The subsidiaries of MNEs also organise seminars or work sessions which supervisory staff from other subsidiaries or from headquarters may attend. In Sri Lanka many MNEs have, in such circumstances, used the aid of the National Institute of Management or other local bodies.

Finally, the role of employers' organisations in the promotion of training becomes more important when the MNEs are strongly represented in them. There is an emphasis on training not only because the MNEs are able to assess training needs, but also because the multinationals have the necessary data and experience to adapt

training to the local context.   The study and training group
GEFDCP (mentioned earlier in this chapter) brings together, for
example, Moroccan personnel directors in order to promote training
and exchange of information in this field.   The instruction
includes seminars, luncheon discussions and other meetings.

External training facilities

The main distinguishing characteristic and the major advantage
which MNEs have over competing national firms in the area of
training is that the MNE is able to seek assistance from the parent
company and other subsidiaries and branches of the group.

During the installation phase the support from the parent
company and other subsidiaries takes the form of technical teaching
aids, instructors and trainers sent to the new plant.   Trainers
are progressively replaced by local personnel.   This procedure is
generally applied, but sometimes different installation practices
prevail.   A notable exception is the "turn-key" industrial project
where the entire staff, from managers to semi-skilled workers, is
brought from abroad to set up the factory.   The absence of trained
national personnel at the time of installation leads later to
numerous maintenance difficulties.

MNEs also make arrangements to give basic and advanced training
abroad to some of their foremen, supervisors and technicians.
Workers are sent abroad to learn when the local training facilities
are inadequate or non-existent and when the techniques to be
learned are specific to that particular enterprise.   In at least
two countries covered by the study the costs of training nationals
abroad may be assumed partially or entirely by the training funds
or organisations in charge of training in the developing nation.
The funds are replenished by the payroll tax.   The government
agrees to finance training abroad when there is a lack of similar
training in the host country.   When the courses are held at a
training centre operated by the parent company, the money which the
enterprise receives from the national fund really amounts to a
refund of some of the taxes paid into that fund by the subsidiary.
National companies, in contrast, have to bear the full cost of
training.

Of the five managers of three Moroccan MNEs training abroad,
three were training at the headquarters of the parent companies
and two were training at other subsidiaries.   In the Ivory Coast,
80 per cent of the requests for training abroad submitted to the
ONFP are for training at company headquarters or at subsidiaries.
With respect to the remaining 20 per cent it is not always clear
if some of the requests relate to training at centres belonging to
the group of companies to which the MNE in question belongs.   The
financing of courses which familiarise the workers with new
machinery might be questioned in this context.   Some of these
costs are often paid by the manufacturer of the new equipment, but
the MNEs still claim a reimbursement from the national training
authority on the grounds that the instruction provides specific
training in the use of the production equipment.

Instances of training abroad seem less frequent in the case of
the two Asian countries studied, Bangladesh and Sri Lanka, as well
as in the case of Costa Rica.   This impression, however, may be the
result of insufficient information.

Finally, the advanced training opportunities offered by some of the large multinational companies should be mentioned. Management candidates who have completed three years of service with the enterprise are nominated for admission to outstanding training institutions in the home country of the parent enterprise. In addition there are more modest fellowships for training abroad offered to foremen and supervisors who have shown particular promise. Those awarded fellowships enjoy the administrative backing of the group or of the headquarters during the period of their studies.

In summary, MNEs and national companies in the countries surveyed are subject to the same conditions and obligations concerning training. However, MNEs enjoy certain advantages because they often belong to a particular sector (i.e. agriculture) and are linked to their parent company and the other subsidiaries (facilitating foreign exchange, arrangements for accommodation, etc.).

The decentralisation of training activities within the MNEs brings their subsidiaries closer into line with national enterprises. Both kinds of enterprises face the same types of problems such as the identification of training needs and the shortage of management cadres, especially supervisory personnel. These problems are not easy to solve because the modern technology used by MNEs calls for high levels of skill. As has been seen, the MNEs are therefore usually obligated to give further instruction in addition to that given by the national training institutions. Such additional training aimed at ensuring better adaptation to the job often results, however, in an excessively specialised worker whose occupational mobility is then reduced. But it would be wrong to generalise in this regard. In fact, the recruitment policies of MNEs are very closely linked to their training policies. Some like to recruit managers and skilled workers who are beginners; others try to encourage career development through internal promotions or favour the recruitment of experienced staff. In all cases there is a problem of turnover and exodus. However, even when national policies encourage the emigration or trained labour, MNEs still contribute to the achievement of this national development goal by training workers.

Although conditions in the countries on which data has been collected differ widely, the replacement of management staff by national cadres continues to follow the objectives laid down by the governments concerned. A sizeable part of the in-plant training and understudy training is given by expatriate managerial or supervisory personnel. Large multinational companies seem to have less difficulty than small companies in replacing their expatriate staff with national workers.

In practice the training best suited to the interests of the MNE is ensured through a combination of its own training resources, local resources (mainly national institutions) and external resources (chiefly those of the headquarters or the group). As far as one can see from the survey undertaken, this combination is based on a close collaboration with national institutions in the training of labourers and skilled workers and on well developed relations with the headquarters for the training of managers and higher grade technicians.

Evaluation of multinational enterprises' training
contribution in co-operation with local institutions

In addition to the implicit collaboration, as outlined in
the section above, MNEs also give direct support, unconnected to
the training of the subsidiary concerned, to the training efforts
of the host country. Direct contributions of various kinds made
by MNEs to the improvement of training of supervisors and workers
may be grouped under two main headings:

- collaboration in the definition of training policies and programmes and the leadership which MNEs can give in preparing
  and launching new training programmes; and

- direct support of training efforts, either by way of material
  or technical assistance.

(i) The special role of MNEs in training

MNEs usually use structures and facilities which enable them
to meet their training needs by collaborating closely with national
and other local training institutes. Such collaboration is
mutually advantageous because the national partners of the MNEs
get the benefit of techniques and ideas used elsewhere. Also,
the co-operation leads to administrative support for national pilot
projects in the preliminary stages.

Collaboration in training policies

One of the three types of national systems referred to at the
beginning of this chapter consists of institutions with tripartite
management or advisory boards (Morocco, Ivory Coast and Nigeria).
The employers' organisations participating in them generally include
representatives of MNE subsidiaries, but as far as can be seen
MNEs as such are not represented. In Morocco only one of the five
enterprises surveyed participates through the Moroccan employers'
confederation, Confédération Générale Economique Morocaine (CGEM),
in the work of the governing board of the ONFP. All five of the
MNEs are, however, invited to participate in the training councils
which monitor changes in the labour market and propose modifications
in the training programmes of the centres on the basis of these
changes.   Two of the MNEs surveyed declined to continue their
participation in these councils because of the meagre results
obtained at such meetings.   This refusal may, to a certain extent,
be considered a form of pressure to secure improvements in the
training machinery.   The training experience acquired by many MNEs
lends a certain weight to the opinions they may express in various
committees even when such opinions, to the regret of some employers
and unions, are of a purely advisory nature.   A similar situation
is found in Costa Rica and Nigeria.

In Costa Rica the co-operation between the INA and the national
or multinational enterprises is practical.   It involves quantitative
and qualitative studies of training needs.   Interestingly, all
the MNEs operating in the country co-operate in these studies and
other efforts.   As a result the INA offers training which addresses
the needs expressed by the enterprises.   One example is the special
study of the quantitative need for additional training in the MNE-
owned banana plantations.   Voluntary, non-statutory employer-worker

liaison committees with INA also exist. Depending on the sector
involved these committees may have an advisory role on questions of
general policy, technical implementation or organisation, promotion
and operation of training programmes.

In Bangladesh the collaboration of the MNEs in the definition
of national training policy continues to be marginal due to the
absence of a central national body responsible for training. The
recent creation of the National Vocational Training Council
suggests, however, that national and multinational enterprises may
participate more closely in the future in the discussions and
decisions relating to the development of training standards and
training policy. Already MNEs have contributed to this type of
activity by making suggestions on draft proposals submitted to them
for their consideration which relate to skill standards. Such
involvement in the advancement of training standards occurs at
three levels:

- the level of national bodies and advisory committees on which
  5 of the 15 MNEs replying to the survey are represented;

- the level of the administrative organs of the institute of
  management and technicians on which 6 of the 19 MNEs replying
  are represented; and

- the level of activities directly tied to training (i.e.
  standards, selection, etc.) in which 6 of the 15 MNEs replying
  to the relevant survey are represented.

In Sri Lanka vocational training is the responsibility of the
government bodies. There it appears that MNEs do not participate
much at the level of forming training policy. Nevertheless,
the governing boards of various institutions such as the Institute
of Management include employers' representatives who are often
from MNEs.

MNEs collaborate formally in the formation of training policy
and programmes through employers' organisations. Informally, and
perhaps more effectively, the MNEs' own training efforts set an
example which has a multiplier effect on other companies.

In each of the national bodies to which ILO technical advisers
are attached there is evidence of the support which the MNEs give
to new and existing programmes. Thus, in the Ivory Coast MNEs
have actively encouraged the drafting and application of the law
on continuous training (where they are in fact the only enterprises
able to offer such training). The larger MNEs, in addition, have
adopted a policy of "Ivorisation" of their personnel. In Costa
Rica the active participation of MNEs in INA programmes and innovations has been noted by the ILO adviser concerned. The expert also
refers to an experiment carried out by an MNE on occupational
certification in electrical maintenance.

Furthermore, MNEs participating in sectoral projects launched
by national institutions guide the project and set standards of
performance, thereby permitting progress while taking into account
various local constraints. At this stage it is perhaps appropriate
to call attention to the essentially decentralised training policy
for MNE subsidiaries: the parent company may define global
objectives and make certain facilities available, but the identification of training needs and the action they call for is the

responsibility of the subsidiary.   Herein lies the need for as
active a contribution as possible by these subsidiaries to local
training efforts.   In Bangladesh, for example, these efforts are
supported and even promoted by the MNEs.

Similarly, when an MNE enters into a contract with a national
training institute or body for training in centres or in the
plants, the national institutions benefit from the experience of
the MNEs.   There are, of course, at least two dangers involved:
excess training capacity in trades which are not in great demand
in the national labour market (a danger being confronted by the
national training office of the Ivory Coast), and a training
monopoly developing to the advantage of multinational and large
national enterprises.   These large firms can then absorb national
training resources to the detriment of small- and medium-size
enterprises.   Thus, in Bangladesh 10 out of the 11 MNEs which
participate in the work of national training bodies or institutes
of management have more than 250 workers.

Certain employers' organisations have pointed out, however,
that because of training regulation funds, a redistribution of
resources in favour of the small- and medium-size enterprises does
occur.   In the Ivory Coast it seems easy for smaller enterprises
to draw benefits in excess of 75 per cent of their contribution to
the training tax and, as a result, to draw on the regulatory fund
which is supported primarily by contributions from the large
companies.   It is probably easier, however, for a large company
than for a small one to identify its training deficiencies.   As a
result, the training requests come more frequently from large
enterprises.

Finally, the special contribution of all MNE training efforts
is that they are long-lasting and that they adapt to the technological changes to which the MNEs are very sensitive.   Furthermore,
MNEs train workers in order to fulfil production goals, an objective which presupposes as long and as stable an operational existence
as possible in the country.   This spirit of continuity, combined
with adjustment to the changing needs of the labour market, is not
necessarily shared by private or public training institutions.
Too often these institutions regard training as an end in itself
or as a sort of routine operation.

(ii)   Assistance provided by MNEs, for the
       advancement of local training programmes

Along with benefiting from local training facilities, MNEs
frequently help these same institutions.   In fact, available
information suggests that MNEs almost invariably respond favourably
to requests from local training facilities for help.   Some of the
MNEs would even volunteer to increase their support if they were
allowed or requested to do so or if the national bodies showed
"better management capacities".

Direct assistance by MNEs to local training institutions takes
various forms and is inspired by a variety of considerations.   Aid
can take the form of technical training or the offer of the use of
facilities, materials, and equipment.   Aid can be monetary grants
as well.   Another form of assistance can be offering training and
educational programmes unconnected with the production needs of the
particular MNE and open to persons inside or outside the enterprise.

If some of these efforts are clearly prompted by the enterprise's sense of social responsibility, other efforts are inspired
by production goals.   Additional reasons for involvement in training
again may reflect the political and economic imperatives or the
requirements of long-term personnel policy.   It would be presump-
tuous at this point to enter into the details of these often overlapping motives since the analytical elements required are missing
anyway.   On the other hand, it would seem useful to list, with the
help of the examples available, the types of assistance practised
by MNEs in the countries covered, together with the conditions
attached to the assistance.   These are:

- social, when their aim is to provide access to, encourage
  information of and promote training in subjects which are not
  directly linked to the production or management techniques
  of the enterprise, e.g. basic skills;

- technical, when the MNE offers to loan its staff or to place
  its courses or teaching materials at the disposal of other
  enterprises or training institutions;   or

- material, when the MNE loans or gives money, equipment or
  facilities.

Basic social training

Many of the multinationals surveyed offer their staff, the
staff's families or any other interested persons, programmes of
general education including courses in reading, technology, and
culture.   Thus, many enterprises encourage their workers to
acquire a general education outside working hours.   The companies
encourage their workers to enrol in courses in languages, logic,
mathematics, etc.   One Moroccan enterprise pays 50 per cent of the
tuition for such courses and reimburses the remaining 50 per cent if
the student successfully completes the course.   The enterprise
hopes, in this way, to encourage the personal development as well
as the horizontal mobility of its staff.   In the Ivory Coast a
request for financing 24 mathematics fellowships has been filed
with the regulatory fund authority.   In Bangladesh, 10 out of 13
enterprises say they provide courses on general culture to their
workers and their workers' families.

The literacy education programmes are offered mainly in rural
areas, especially at the plantations.   In the Ivory Coast, one MNE
of this type runs a programme of literacy training, hygiene and home
economics in addition to other school subjects.[1]   The courses are
offered to residents of the plantation villages[1] as well as to
company employees and their families.   Such community development
programmes are not undertaken exclusively by MNEs.   State enterprises such as mines or plantations also conduct similar programmes.

---

[1] These are villages of landed proprietors who harvest their
own crop but have signed contracts with MNEs for its sale.   The
MNEs also contract to assist the proprietors with technical
training.   Each proprietor may have one or more kind of
plantation (e.g. cocoa, rubber, palms), the produce of which may
be contracted to different buyers.

Although the technical and managerial training which MNEs
provide to the small national enterprises which handle distribution
or maintenance of their products is principally for the MNEs'
benefit, the training does raise the level of skills in the country.
In the automobile sector, for example, it is not unusual to find
workers or foremen leaving an MNE to open repair garages with the
financial and technical backing of that company. One subsidiary
of an automobile manufacturer included in the survey devotes part
of its training activities to spreading management techniques among
the small enterprises representing its make. This type of training
is also extended to users of products. For example, a tyre
manufacturer organises quarterly seminars for its distributing
agents, training courses for garage mechanics and other training
courses for the mechanics of large, public or private transport
companies.

MNEs offer training facilities to local agricultural or
industrial entrepreneurs who supply raw materials or semi-finished
goods or who finish the MNEs' products. Though this training
contributes to the economic and social development of the host
country there still are the risks of monopoly or monopsony. The
MNE, as sole buyer or seller, may impose its technical or financial
terms on the small local enterprises. Furthermore, the training
offered by the MNE to small entrepreneurs is generally very
specific, and there are tendencies to keep the transfer of technology to a strict minimum. This specificity of training has
frequently been found in the countries examined. Examples include
the training of banana producers in Costa Rica and of rubber
planters in the Ivory Coast.

Nevertheless, in two of the countries studied small- and
medium-size enterprises are being absorbed and are disappearing
as the MNEs expand their activities. Some of the people interviewed therefore see certain training policies of MNE subsidiaries
as a means of pressuring the small- and medium-size enterprises
economically linked to them.

Technical support

Some of the MNEs sampled for this study declare that their
training facilities are open to people not working for their
enterprises. Frequent mention is made regarding the admission of
trainees from engineering or management schools and from national
vocational training schools. Thus, in Bangladesh, 5 enterprises
out of 18 replying to this question accept such graduates for in-
plant training, and 7 other enterprises permit trainees to acquire
practical experience in their workshops. Four enterprises
belonging to the chemical industries sector combine the two types
of training. Three of the enterprises in question employ between
450 and 500 workers while the fourth has only 16. One MNE in
Guinea accepted 45 trainees in 1972. Some enterprises which play
a pilot role in training in the host countries do not hesitate to
open their centres to trainees from other enterprises, even if these
are rival companies. Such is the case, to give one example, of a
multinational sugar refinery. Furthermore, there are MNEs which
offer places in their training courses to individual candidates or
candidates suggested by other enterprises. Such practices, of
course, widen the field of selection of the MNEs, but there are
often other considerations behind such admissions, such as the need,
for pedagogic reasons, to obtain a minimum number of students in a

course.   One multinational company has a training centre for
welding which, for a fee, will accept workers from other enterprises.

Temporary detachment or exchange of trainers is a fairly
frequent practice, either to assist a centre or institute or to
provide training in special fields.   Thus, in Sri Lanka a number
of directors or managers from MNEs run courses or occasionally
lecture at the National Institute for Business Management.   In
Bangladesh 8 out of 20 multinational enterprises surveyed state
that they supply instructors and lecturers to national training
institutions.   One MNE in Morocco indicates that it organises
information and technical courses to update instructors who teach
subjects connected with the use of its products.

Material assistance

Financial support to governmental institutions beyond the
payment of taxes seems to be a somewhat rare form of MNE co-
operation in national training efforts.   However, given the size
of MNEs in the countries surveyed, the total amount of training
taxes paid by them is larger than that paid by national enterprises
as a whole.   Naturally two situations can arise: either the
training expenditure exceeds the amount paid into the training fund
or, on the contrary, contributions to the fund exceed the expenses
reimbursed.

In the first case, the MNE reaps the benefit of contributions
made by other enterprises.   One extreme case has been mentioned
(Costa Rica) where MNEs belonging to a tax-free sector benefit from
training facilities financed by other, largely national, sectors.
On the other hand, sometimes the benefits which the MNEs receive
are offset by the firms' own training programmes which are open to
workers from outside the enterprises (e.g. Morocco).

In the second possibility the MNEs contribute indirectly to
the financing of training for small- and medium-size enterprises
(Ivory Coast, Nigeria, Morocco).

Specific financial support by multinational enterprises for
the construction of centres or for the organisation of seminars and
short training courses is reported in particular in Sri Lanka and
Bangladesh but appears to be fairly prevalent in the other
countries studied.

With regard to providing equipment, including audio-visual
aids, machine tools or office equipment, there are two main trends:
(a) the donations of new and up-to-date equipment;   and (b) the
donations of second-hand or obsolete material.

When MNEs supply new equipment adaptable to training aids, the
donation bears a greater resemblance to trade promotion than to
disinterested assistance.   Beyond a doubt, when an MNE supplies
a certain machine, the enterprise assumes that the person trained
in its use will continue to use this particular piece of equipment.
However, only one example of this type of gift has come to the
attention of the experts interviewed for this study.   The more
frequent practice seems to be the donation of used or obsolete
equipment which, although perfectly suited to training activities,
is not tied to the current production programme of any particular

multinational.   The practice most frequently encountered is the
supply of power equipment to mechanical training centres, but the
donation of motor vehicles for the transport of trainees and of
radio and television equipment for courses using them has also been
reported in Bangladesh.

One reported case, which unfortunately does not appear to be
unique, is the disappointing experience faced by an enterprise in
offering materials.   A large gift of equipment was first not
picked up - as had been arranged - by the training centre in
question.   The MNE donating the equipment then had to deliver it.
Subsequently the use of some of the equipment was abandoned when
the oil needed to be changed or when the machines needed a minimum
amount of maintenance.

In one of the countries surveyed one training officer declared
that, to his knowledge, no gift of equipment could be accepted by
the training centres despite their acute needs in this field.
Paradoxically, because of the import tax exemption, the public body
responsible for training imports the material required to equip the
training centres of the MNEs.

Similarly, the premises, the workshops and the facilities of
enterprises visited are made available by the MNE.   These centres
are sometimes underutilised, even though the majority of the enterprises surveyed offer this type of assistance.   There are
apparently many cases similar to that of Bangladesh where 7 enterprises out of 20 are ready to increase their aid, particularly for
the development of inter-enterprise activities.   In Costa Rica
the ILO team of experts and the INA report that they have made good
use of the workshops and classrooms provided by MNEs.   The
facilities have been used both for conducting courses and for
holding qualifying examinations for skills certificates.   Sometimes
the course materials have been printed by the MNEs.   Similar
assistance was received by the ILO team attached to the Bangladesh
project.   Confronted with delays in the delivery of training
equipment, the ILO team was loaned workshops, classrooms and
reproduction and printing facilities by at least two MNEs.   Some
of these facilities continue to be available even though the project
is now fully operational.

Formal collaboration of the MNEs in the framing of a training
policy takes place when permitted by the national institutional
structure, at the level of the governing or advisory boards of
national, regional, or occupational bodies.   The MNEs as such are
rarely represented on these bodies.   Instead, MNEs are represented
as members of employers' or professional organisations.   Func-
tionally, the training structures and practices of MNEs often permit
close collaboration with national training institutions, particularly
in commencing new programmes or in conducting basic research on such
matters as skill certification and training needs.

The direct spppport of most MNEs to the national training efforts
to develop training takes different shapes depending on the relations with national training institutions.   The aid may consist of
assistance in raising the standard of general education, in technical
training or in placing training staff and equipment at the disposal
of national bodies.   All such assistance is usually linked with

the more or less long-term interests of the enterprise. These
interests relate to recruitment, budget management, training,
industrial relations, marketing and supplies, etc. However,
whatever the MNE's motivations might be, the results of such
collaboration are apparently beneficial primarily to the host
country. Some of the government officials, employers and MNEs
interviewed therefore seem to think that the scope of greater
collaboration with MNEs should be further explored by national
employers' or training organisations.

Concluding observations

Some conclusions concerning the fields and conditions of co-
operation between national institutions and multinational enterprises in the area of training can be drawn from the analysis of
the situations described above.

In the first instance one might reflect upon whether there
are differences between the training practices of MNEs and the
training offered by large domestic enterprises (public or private).
A comprehensive study might possibly have uncovered some variations
in training efforts. A priori it could have been expected that one
of the advantages of MNEs - in addition to the advanced training
techniques which they have developed - would lie in their capacity
to give informal training as well (i.e. that over and above
formal courses and seminars) which originates from what can be
called the "business culture". This prevailing ethos allows the
employee to acquire values, while working in the enterprise,
which complement his formal training through actual experience in
areas related to logic, punctuality, productivity, rigour, quality
control and safety. Such advantages, however, are not specific to
MNEs. In fact, informal training is offered neither exclusively
nor automatically by MNEs and it would be interesting to note
factors favourable to creating the conditions under which MNEs
offer such training.

Secondly, there is often the difference of goals which is
referred to: the multinationals train workers in order to facilitate immediate growth. National institutions, on the contrary,
are concerned with multifaceted training corresponding to the
needs of development. Raising the problem in these terms would
necessitate more research than was possible in this study. It
would mean a detailed study, especially of the known controversy
on the relative merits of in-plant training versus training
centres. One may however point out that the necessity for skill
training on the job is frequently a consequence of inadequate
basic local training, and that there are many examples of the
complementary training given by the institutions and the
enterprises.

The many forms of training sometimes observed in enterprises
in the public sector may contrast with the more specialised training
found in multinationals. However, the reasons for this need to be
recalled since they may affect the manner in which the training
practices of the MNEs can be integrated into the various national
systems. First, public sector enterprises are often closely tied
to the national development plan and thus mainly reflect the social
and economic goals of the government. Moreover, these plans endow
public enterprises with a leadership role. Second, public sector

enterprises sometimes have to compensate for their relatively low pay scales with other advantages such as opportunities for training and for internal advancement. Finally, one notes that the proportion of MNEs that encourage diverse training tends to be higher where the employment market is more rigid. In this case they are able to encourage internal promotion without much risk of increased manpower turnover.

Is there, then, really an important difference in the training goals of MNEs and public institutions? The difference is no greater than that between private national firms and official training institutions in any country. A major problem in developing countries is the weakness of their national training structures in comparison with the more experienced, better equipped and more specialised structures of the MNEs. Some of the examples of co-operation cited earlier point to possibilities of mutually complementary efforts that may be worth further exploration.

As far as one can judge from the examples available, the potential for technical, social and material support has often been underestimated and underutilised by authorities of developing countries. Also underestimated is the good example of the multi-nationals and their influence on training in national enterprises and national institutions. In certain cases administrative or purely political considerations prevent the donation of material or other training aids by MNEs. While respecting the political choices of the countries, one may still regret that a country may not benefit from potential resources through lack of better administrative co-ordination or through faulty understanding of the comparative advantages of the MNEs.

It is also possible to gain the impression, from the examples cited, that the measures taken by governments to encourage training reflect their concern with specific problems rather than with an over-all training policy. This is particularly true with regard to the governmental "indigenisation" or the emigration policies when the implications for the over-all training system are not always fully considered. The absence of training cadres and clear objectives naturally leads to a certain amount of overlapping and waste of resources. MNEs, for example, hire the best instructors of the training institutions. Also, managers and supervisors trained at great cost by the national institutions either are absorbed by the MNEs or have to hunt for jobs which require them to undergo more training.

Of course, it is difficult to avoid some overlap between the training given by the official institutions and by the MNEs. However, it should be possible to define within each country a framework for co-operation for the various training bodies with a precise role for multinationals. In the formation of national training policies MNEs can provide guidance if they can expect assistance from local institutions and if the contribution of these MNEs is more clearly defined.

CHAPTER IV

THREE CASE STUDIES ON THE IMPACT OF TRAINING
BY MULTINATIONALS ON DEVELOPMENT[1]

A CASE STUDY ON TRAINING PRACTICES OF MULTI-
NATIONAL ENTERPRISES IN BRAZIL

by

Cláudio de Moura Castro[2] and
Sandra Ma. C. de Sá Carneiro

The importance of multinationals
in the manufacturing sector

The Brazilian industrial sector has presented, during the
past years, a remarkable growth and has in this process become
the most dynamic sector of the economy as a whole. In fact,
during the period 1970-77, its real product showed a 101.4 per
cent increase as compared to 98.4 per cent in the transport/
communication sector, 87.7 per cent in trade and 53.8 per cent
in agriculture.

The great importance of the industrial sector in the
Brazilian economy appears clearly in the composition of the 1977
net national product, of which 12 per cent is attributed to agriculture, 37 per cent to industry and 51 per cent to services
(estimates). The net contribution of the industrial sector to
the national product thus exceeds the contribution of the agricultural sector. In general we can assert that today Brazil has
a mature industrial sector within which the most important subsector is represented by the manufacturing industries which
generate more than 70 per cent of the domestic product of the
whole sector.

As a most important feature in this industrial growth, the
role of multinational enterprises, must be emphasised. In fact
in 1977, of the 200 major corporations (not including finance)
operating in the economy, 45 were foreign, 66 domestic private
and 89 state owned. Although the number of multinational enterprises (MNEs) is relatively low, their economic importance is
considerable, as the following chart shows.

---

[1] See the guidelines prepared for the authors of the case
studies providing structural and procedural instructions in an
attempt to facilitate comparability (which are reproduced in the
annex).

[2] Technical Project Co-ordinator, Programme for Joint
Studies on Latin American Integration (ECIEL), Brazil. We
would like to thank Ricardo Chaves de Rezende Martins for his
co-operation in this work.

The responsibility for opinions expressed in this contribution rests solely with the authors.

Importance of MNEs in the Brazilian
manufacturing industry
(percentages)

Firms	Net assets	Earnings	Net profit	Employment
State-owned	73	41	56	44
Domestic private	14	21	22	31
Multinationals	13	38	22	25
Total	100	100	100	100

Source: Compilation by the authors.

The capital of the multinational enterprises equals that of
the domestic private firms. However, the earnings of the
multinationals are much higher, almost as high as those of the
public firms. Their profit is as high as that of the private
enterprises and they employ an appreciable share of the labour
force in the manufacturing industry.

The contribution of multinational enterprises to the technological development of Brazil has been diverse. The enterprises control activities in which the main technical progress
occurs and where the flow of new products is most intense, i.e.
durable consumer goods and capital equipment. It needs to be
pointed out, however, that the competitiveness of the Brazilian
industry depends to a certain extent on the intensity of the
transfer of technical progress as it takes place within the
multinational enterprises.

The main objective of this case study is to shed light on
the training practices of multinational enterprises in Brazil as
compared to the training practices of large public corporations
there. As will be seen, some training differences can indeed
be detected between both categories of firms, although they are
not obvious initially.

Sampling design for the
case study

For the purpose of this study a sample of five multinational
and public enterprises have been selected from the Rio de Janeiro
region where 56 of the 200 largest Brazilian firms are located.
Three major multinational enterprises were included in the sample.
All these three enterprises had been part of a sample of firms
surveyed for the first time by the authors seven years ago.
Returning to them for the present case study gave the authors a
good comparative view over time. The five enterprises of the
sample, three of which are multinational and two public, have the
following characteristics:

Enterprise A is of American origin and operates in the electro-
mechanical sector. It employs 4,300 people, 80 per cent of them
working in production lines. Established in Brazil 58 years ago,

its activities are concentrated in two plants in São Paulo, one
in Rio, two plants in Minas Gerais and one in Recife.   In 1977
it ranked 130th in terms of assets, and 45th in earnings.
Within the electro-mechanical subsector, its Recife plant ranks
25th in all Brazil.

Enterprise B is of European origin.   It manufactures telecommunication and electrical equipment.   Its size equals that
of firm A.   Nearly 70 per cent of its personnel operate directly
in the production process.   Established in Brazil more than
50 years ago, the enterprise has two industrial plants, one in
Rio de Janeiro and one in Minas Gerais.   Within the electrical
material subsector, it ranks fourth in assets and fifth in
earnings.   The four largest firms in this subsector are multinationals.

Enterprise C is of Japanese origin.   It operates in the
area of heavy equipment and employs approximately 5,000 people.
The enterprise started its activities 20 years ago and has two
large plants in Rio, and 70 per cent of its staff is engaged in
production work.   The enterprise holds the 128th place in assets
and within the naval construction subsector ranked fourth,
although presenting the highest net profit in 1977.   In this
subsector, the three largest firms are private.

Enterprise D is a public transportation company (Interstate
Railroad System) and employs 95,000 people.   It is the fourth
largest Brazilian firm and first in terms of assets within the
subsector of railroads.   In 1977 it ranked 28th in earnings in
the country.

Enterprise E is an oil company.   Founded in 1953 it has a
total of 5,300 employees.   It has six subsidiaries, a synthetic
rubber plant and three large petrochemical plants.   It is the
largest company in the country with the highest assets and
revenues inside and outside the oil and derivatives subgroup.

The five enterprises included in the sample show great
variety in the composition of their labour force and require a
considerable number of skilled workers.   All these firms invest
heavily in equipment, which is expected of firms of this size.

Previous knowledge of the firms was an important consideration in defining the sample;   another set of firms would have
meant less information.   But again, the factors that influenced
the sampling design of the original research must be recalled.
This was the best large-firm sample that could be obtained on
that occasion.   Some alternative choices were reluctant to go
along with the survey, and Rio de Janeiro after all, does not
have that many alternatives.   The railroad firm may seem a
strange choice but one must remember that we are examining their
maintenance yards.   The tasks are typical of those found in the
mechanical industry.   And, in addition, railroads have been the
pioneers - both in Rio and São Paulo - of technical and vocational
training in Brazil.   Indeed, SENAI[1] originated that way in
São Paulo in the 1930s.

---

[1] SENAI (Serviço Nacional de Apprendizagem Industrial) stands
for the National Service of Industrial Apprenticeship, a very
large and important training organisation.

The absence of private Brazilian firms from the sample is regrettable but meaningful.   No comparable Brazilian private firm could be identified in Rio.   Although they do exist, big business is dominated by multinationals and public firms.   In contrast to a good part of the civil service, public firms are aggressive, invest heavily, recruit competitively in the market and pay well.

The characteristics of case studies should always be kept in mind.   As it ought to be, the authors do not claim the results to be generally valid or applicable in every other case.   But again, what makes case studies interesting is an implicit assumption that things are probably not that different in other firms. In fact, some of the results are known to be quite general although evidence for these findings may be coincidental.

Expatriate staff in the multi-nationals

While examining the labour composition of the multinationals, we observed a low number of foreigners in their ranks.   The highest proportion observed in one enterprise was 3 per cent. The other two MNEs show much lower percentages of foreigners. In general, key positions of these firms are held by foreigners, mostly at the middle and high-managerial levels.   In the lower echelons, those processes which are significantly different from the usual industrial practices are temporarily managed by foreigners, and then taken over by local personnel after a sufficient training period.

When the three multinational enterprises established them-selves in Brazil, the technicians and management staff were foreigners.   At present, multinationals seem to rely mostly on the training abroad of high-level technicians and managers of Brazilian origin.   Such training at headquarters is considered more productive because of the opportunity of "hands on" practice on the equipment to be introduced in the local subsidiaries. Apart from this, all other training afforded by the enterprises is organised by Brazilians.   This approach avoids the main problem of foreign technicians or instructors in Brazil, i.e. "culture shock".   Foreign instructors are accustomed to an entirely different environment and meet considerable problems in trying to introduce local workers to new working methods and procedures.   Thus, enterprise C sent nearly 160 employees, from department managers to skilled workers, to headquarters for training during the period 1970-77.   During the same period, the number of foreign technicians in Brazil was insignificant.   In general, they remain for a period of five years until local per-sonnel have been trained.

An important point to be emphasised is the fact that because personnel managers and training supervisors are mainly Brazilian, they display a considerable degree of job mobility changing frequently from multinational to domestic public or private firms. Many of these managers started as instructors in a multinational enterprise, became supervisors in another enterprise, and may now be human resource managers in a third one.

The process of transferring technology

One immediate inference of the training policies referred
to is that production is basically in the hands of Brazilians.
Hence, the problem of transfer of technology[1] via multinationals
seems to have a mechanical and simple answer taking also into
consideration that the number of expatriates is insignificant.

This transfer happens progressively. It is paced by the
nature of the production processes, generally imported from
abroad when a technology is adopted. When the nature of the
productive process at headquarters is different from the one
commonly utilised locally, then technology will be transferred,
to the extent that local workers can be trained to use the new
technology. The skill acquired by them in this connection is
frequently simple ability or manual skills, which they did not
possess when frequently they were hired.

The transfer of technology is dictated by the existence of
a technology gap between headquarters and local practices in
Brazil. When this gap exists, the transfer takes place. Consequently workers are trained when a new technology is introduced.
In this sense, training decisions play a passive role. Firms
differ in technology but not in their policy to always train
local workers to utilise the technology necessary for the production process in the Brazilian subsidiaries. The level of
mastery of the imported technology is variable. At first
workers in routine operations are trained; then local maintenance crews replace expatriates first used for this work; and
higher echelons are replaced later.

It is interesting to note, however, that today the greater
part of the machinery used in the productive process of the
multinationals is manufactured in Brazil. None of the surveyed
multinational enterprises had less than 70 per cent Brazilian
machinery components. Some of this equipment produced in Brazil
is already exported to other branches of the multinational enterprise outside the country.

---

[1] For the purposes of the present case study, transfer of
technology must be understood in a very broad way. Developing
computer circuitry is a typical area in which the expression is
used in recent discussions. However, when we examine training
as a vehicle for technology transfer, such ambitious definitions
would not be meaningful. Learning to wire and test a computer
component is understood here as transfer of technology if the
procedure was imported from abroad. More generally, organisational and procedure skills may be one of the most important
aspects of this transfer. Organisation of work, production
control, quality control and some kind of "technical culture" may
be the longer-lasting aspects of this technology transfer imported
through training.

A good example of the process of technology transfer is furnished by enterprise B. During the first decade after its establishment in Brazil, the firm imported all of its machinery and equipment. Local personnel were merely in charge of assembling and the operation and maintenance of the imported equipment. After these first ten years, the production in Brazil of small machinery and parts was initiated. Finally, 50 per cent of the machinery and spare parts was manufactured in Brazil. By this time enterprise B manufactured in Brazil home appliances and electric and telecommunications equipment. In the meantime, while the production of communication material increased, that of home appliances diminished until it was discontinued in 1968. One of the main reasons for this was the Brazilian Government's support - through financial and fiscal incentives - of the expansion of the country's telephone network favouring also the enterprises telecommunication production line.

The methods of preparing workers for new technological processes vary with circumstances. Thus manuals and technical bulletins are frequently translated and adapted to local conditions. In the case of more complex technologies, greater planning and anticipation is required. For instance, enterprise B is in the process of preparing its assembly lines for a new product. This will be carried out in stages and it is believed that by the end of 1980 the reconversion will be completed. For the acquisition of the sophisticated know-how required in this connection personnel at managerial level and technicians are being sent to Spain and France.

Training opportunities offered by the Government and training strategies adopted by the multinationals

When we examined the training strategies of each firm, we find that they are the result of simple and logical decisions.

One of the main problems facing Brazilian industry is the poor qualification of its labour force. Due to this factor, the enterprises are forced to prepare and train, themselves, most of their workers. As a consequence, we observe that a large part of the workers' training occurs only after the individual has entered the firm. In general, enterprises in Brazil do not look for formally trained labour, but for "trainable" people. They then try to give priority to training (with adequate preparation in the required quantity) in those areas in which a sufficient number of qualified workers are not available.

All the enterprises surveyed consider the operational and technical areas as training priorities. Each one of them has its own pattern of labour utilisation at these levels. According to the opinions of department managers of the surveyed firms: "training by itself should not be considered an objective, but one of the tools that can help industries to reach its planned results in terms of production and performance, within a pattern of quality, quantity and cost". In addition, the enterprises feel that the objectives of training can only be achieved when courses, programmes and plans represent the real operational needs of the firm.

In general, we find that there is no particular model of a training programme applicable to any firm. Historical factors, origin, budget and previous training policies seem to dictate the moves necessary at each stage in the development of the enterprise. To evaluate training needs and the establishment of priorities the plant managers are consulted, as are the supervisors of groups and sections within the factory, i.e. internal surveys are made to detect the areas or sectors in need of additional training.

We found that both national and multinational firms approach training as a necessity for their efficient functioning. However, training activities in the multinational enterprises are more dynamic and more oriented towards specialisation. The multinationals in question consider training a worthwhile investment, if the returns are sufficiently high, that is, the increase in productivity can be expected to compensate the cost of training.

On the contrary, the public firms surveyed act on the premise that they must train their personnel in order to improve the level of their qualifications. The courses offered by them tend to be of a general nature, including secondary education and liberal arts-type college degrees. This results in the development of training programmes that do not necessarily correspond to deficiencies detected in the operation of the firm and that entail higher levels of expenditures than the training programmes of multinational enterprises. Employees in public firms seem to have a wider margin of freedom to attend courses, not all of which are justified in terms of increasing personal qualifications or corresponding to real operational needs of the firm. As a result, those firms end up training beyond their own necessities thereby creating problems of excess qualification in several areas. It gives, however, the enterprises a chance to be more selective with regard to the promotion of the trainees.

In general, the multinational enterprises train for optimum performance in the firm while public firms train to increase the educational level of its labour force without considering the possibilities for a more complete utilisation of the trained workers; in this sense, they train more than the multinational enterprises for the economy as a whole and not only for their own needs. Public enterprise D, for example, maintains several training schools. Because of their remuneration policy (wages are low in relation to the market) the enterprise ends up losing a great part of its trained labour (the enterprise has 23 centres of professional training in the country, 18 of which include industrial apprenticeship).

In general, all the surveyed enterprises find it difficult to plan their training programmes systematically because at the time of execution unexpected needs turn up requiring substantial changes of original plans. Sometimes, "extra-programming" amounts to more than what was originally planned. This happens more often with public firms.

Another point worth mentioning is that the multinationals surveyed do not seem to behave completely as could have been predicted through an application of G. Becker's[1] theories which

---

[1] See Gary S. Becker: Human Capital: A Theoretical and Empirical Analysis, with Special Reference to Education (New York, 1975), second edition, pp. 19 ff.

postulate that firms would usually finance only "specific" training, i.e. training useful only for that particular firm. On the contrary, a great part of training by the multinational enterprises tends to be "general" in the sense that it is also useful to the competitors. Is this irrational behaviour? Probably not. If firms cannot find in the market what they need they will train. However, they choose for training workers who have demonstrated that they possess a certain degree of efficiency and job stability to justify an investment.

The labour market is not a perfectly competitive market. Workers do not move instantly to accept a higher offer. Some of them do not have to be that well paid to stay. Hence, enterprises seem to believe that it is worthwhile to train and share the results with others. We can infer this by the fact that there is heavy expenditure in "general" training in the sense used by Becker.

Training patterns for semi-skilled labour

When we compare the multinationals and national enterprises surveyed we find that the differences in training patterns and utilisation depend on the level of skills considered. Depending on the skill level we refer to (manual skill, technicians in middle level, etc.) the pattern is very different. Hardly any generalisation can apply to all levels.

The training usually offered by the enterprises for personnel directly used on the assembly lines emphasises "learning by doing". It simply deals with control over certain production operations or sequences of operations, whether they are physical (dexterity, motor co-ordination) or mental.

There are, however, certain variations in relation to this type of training worth mentioning: enterprise A adopts "on-the-job training" for practically all its workers on the assembly line. These programmes given on-site do not require the frequent use of classrooms, nor time exclusive for training. The cost is zero, as it is simply an unavoidable concomitant of the productive process. Enterprises B and C believe that "on-the-job training" has been made obsolete by other methods since it results in a decrease in productivity and quality. They prefer the use of well-equipped classrooms with the same machines found in the production line for training new workers before they are sent to the factory floor. Enterprise B only abandoned "on-the-job training" in 1976 when an internal campaign called "zero defect" was launched having the purpose of increasing productivity and quality by offering prizes to those sectors reaching certain levels of quality and productivity. Enterprise C does not have assembly lines in the conventional sense and the workers' tasks are more complex. Consequently, a higher level of training is required from all its workers. They operate their own school for that purpose, training personnel in priority areas. All new workers attend this programme (i.e. nearly 70 per cent of the production workers).

In general it is difficult to offer sophisticated training to production line personnel due to their low level of schooling (an average of four years). What can be expected from them is merely the learning of a simple task, for instance, operation of a power machine. As turnover for production workers is very high,

the enterprises do not foresee long training periods because
they consider such training a low-investment return.   In
addition, highly skilled individuals do not easily adapt to
routine tasks of production lines.   At the end of a few weeks
the worker has received adequate training for the set of manual
operations needed and in case he does not meet a given standard
he will be dismissed.   There are a large number of women (nearly
80 per cent) working in production lines of semi-automated
industries as in the case of enterprises A and B.   Due to the
high degree of routine work involved, training managers believe
women can adapt better to this type of activity.   It is said in
particular that due to their patterns of socialisation women are
more apt for sequencial tasks, similar to domestic chores.

Given the nature of the products and the scale of manufacturing, the productive process in enterprises A and B are similar
in terms of labour qualification.   The enterprises display a
great proportion of semi-skilled workers and a moderate number of
highly skilled labour in charge of adjustment, assembly and maintenance of equipment.   For the semi-skilled personnel with a
slightly higher level of schooling than the average and a minimum
of proven competence, a large number of programmes are offered.
These seem to be highly advantageous to the firms, particularly
those with semi-automated operations.   This type of training
develops a (Becker) "specific" knowledge in the sense that they
qualify only in a very specific operation not found in other firms.

The training of skilled labour

For many people, the word "training" brings to mind the
preparation of workers for high-skill manual occupations such as
machinists, electricians, lathe operators, etc.   The training
for those occupations has a long history, both in the traditional
apprentice models and in more structured programmes such as
offered by the Brazilian SENAI (the National Apprenticeship
Service mentioned earlier).   Such training, in addition to
dexterity, motor skills and technical information, requires a
higher conceptual development.   The better conceived and more
structured forms not only teach "how to do" but lead the trainee
to "learn how to learn".

Of all types of training required for manufacturing activities training for skilled labour may be considered as the most
technically developed and the one with deepest impact in the lives
of the trainees.   Programmes preparing semi-skilled workers for
assembly lines or repetitive operations do not amount to much, be
it in duration or depth of social or economic consequence for the
workers.   Equally, engineers, technicians and executives have
followed formal courses too long so as not to be influenced
appreciably by any single further course of study.   However, this
is not so with the skilled worker who may become the "blue-collar
elite".   They acquire, and will subsequently incarnate the values
and ethics of complex manual skills.   Their highest achievements
in abstraction will be obtained as they "marry" physical operations
with the laws of physics; as they immerse themselves in technology.   Even their personality is affected by becoming thus the
equivalent of a member of a professional guild.

As already indicated, the training of skilled workers has
a long tradition in Brazil.[1] SENAI was founded in 1942 by the
Confederation of Industries and the Labour Ministry. In a
country with relatively few distinctions in the area of education,
SENAI may be considered a shining exception.

SENAI's methods and performance can be evaluated in terms of
its international prestige. It serves, indeed, as a model to
other similar institutions in several countries in Latin America
and Africa. Utilising the best available technology and well-
trained instructors, SENAI operates with a wide profile and a
variety of formats. A good part of its programmes are offered
in its own schools, both for apprentices (14 to 18 years of age)
and adults already employed. Under agreements with the Labour
Ministry, programmes for the unemployed are offered. And of
course, SENAI trains instructors for its own purposes as well as
for firms.

However, a considerable part of SENAI activities are conducted inside the firms at their request and sponsored by legal
incentives (rebate on the payroll tax or the more recently introduced income tax deductions). Some of these programmes are a
mere repetition of the school versions; others are adapted to
the specific requirements of the respective enterprises. Two
important points need to be mentioned as interim conclusions:
(a) both national and multinational firms use widely the services
of SENAI, there being no evidence that it is considered a less
desirable alternative by either; and (b) the enterprises do not
duplicate SENAI training in the areas in which it operates.

At present, graduates of SENAI find a very receptive market
given the fast manufacturing growth. Conceivably they could be
hired by firms of any size. No reliable data are available to
indicate their distribution by firm size or ownership. However,
initial data from São Paulo suggests that small firms may hire
proportionately less SENAI graduates than their contributions to
it: in that respect the distribution is regressive. Between
medium and large firms it seems that the medium ones hire proportionately more from the SENAI streamlined programmes while
the big firms favour the graduate of the tailor-made programmes
of SENAI. In São Paulo multinationals are predominantly in
this last category.

Innovation or variation brought by multinational enterprises
in the area of SENAI training seems to be seldom. However,
depending on the particular requirements of each firm, sometimes
the enterprises need staff with further qualifications or workers
with more industrial experience than can be acquired by SENAI
students during their training period. Thus, we find among the
courses offered by multinationals some that merely supplement the
training obtained from SENAI. When enterprise C was established
in the country, it could not find among the Brazilian naval construction the required labourers acquainted with the enterprise's
original tradition (Japanese). The enterprise created, therefore,
its own school with technology, training styles and instructors
brought from Japan.

---

[1] A manufacturer's board.

At present there are two types of basic programmes in this
school: one for trainees recruited without qualifications and
training is offered in welding for three months. For the other,
machinist graduates from SENAI are taken for a supplementary
training period of four months. Only after this training are
the workers introduced to the production process. According to
the training supervisor of enterprise C "it is not wise to recruit,
for example, a welder trained at SENAI because his technical
training has been quite different than that used by the firm.
It would be necessary to train him again; and in some cases this
is not advantageous due to the wide differences in the type of
welding used here".

Despite SENAI's technology and methods being quite up to date
obviously not all needs of the firms can be satisfied by this
institution. Special individual needs can naturally never be
met by any training agency. Indeed the function of SENAI cannot
be seen in satisfying all possible requirements for specific
positions in enterprises.

Still, there is sample evidence that SENAI systematically
offers programmes of high quality and well tuned to the needs of
Brazilian industry. Admittedly, this statement certainly goes
beyond the frame of our sample. The most frequent criticism
concerns a lack of greater specificity in the skills required
for utilising the equipment found in the firms. This comment
must be taken in its proper perspective. Industry needs sound
training in basic skills - which SENAI offers - but individual
firms would prefer what is best for them, not for industry as a
whole, namely, very minute instructions on how to operate their
own machines.

Graduates from SENAI - and that applies to "tecnicos"[1] as
well - receive a broad and general preparation within the boundaries of an occupation. Once in the labour market they are
able to adapt themselves relatively quickly to real-life conditions. In most of the firms, however, we found in the case
of some occupations that rather than acquiring the additional
training on the job, special programmes were sometimes organised,
as for instance, in tool and die-making.

The importance of SENAI is that it provides a wide and sound
"basic training" of the industrial working force. Specific
demands, according to particular business needs, can be fulfilled
by **complementing** SENAI training through programmes of greater
depth or specificity. Such complementary training often takes
place immediately after the recruitment of workers by the enterprise, sometimes in collaboration with SENAI programmes. Skilled
workers who are to be promoted to supervisors very frequently have
to attend a course in leadership and supervision. SENAI has had
much experience in such programmes and has its own package courses
and instructors for this purpose. However, there is a clear
tendency for enterprises to develop their own in-house capacity
to conduct such programmes, and they often utilise former SENAI
instructors in this connection.

---

[1] The concept of "tecnicos" is examined in more detail later
in this case study.

In the official selection and hiring policies of the
enterprises there is no explicit preference for SENAI-trained
workers, a fact confirmed also in our interviews with personnel
officers. For their vacancies, the enterprises simply state
th required skill and experience desired (whenever acquired).
Nevertheless we have found that a very large proportion of workers
in the sample enterprises have been formerly trained by SENAI.
Enterprises A and B prefer to bid in the market for the fully
mature workers rather than to supplement the training of somewhat
less-experienced ones.

SENAI instructors' methods, materials programmes and strategies have permeated through all areas of skilled labour training
both in Brazilian and in multinational firms. SENAI operations
today are clear-cut and can be inferred from their costs and
budget counterparts. But that is only a small part of their
influence. We observed that its heritage was omnipresent in the
firms visited. Our impression was that firms accept this leadership as a fact of life and prefer to concentrate their creative
efforts in other areas.

The industrial "tecnicos"

A very prevalent format of technical training in which
academic subjects are combined with technological courses is the
secondary-level technical schools. In addition, some shop
training is added. Educators have pushed vigorously for this
approach, however, more on the basis of a priori expectations
than of a clearly perceived market demand. The graduates of the
schools in question are not expected to become skilled workers
but supervisors or middle-echelon technical cadres. In depth,
research about this professional category has led to some per-
plexity. Its results are erratic and seem to follow no obvious
patterns. Our research tends to confirm the generally erratic
situation; but we can offer some systematic ideas. The multinational enterprises do not only differ from national firms
regarding patterns of utilisation of technicians, but they differ
also between themselves in this respect. According to their
origin and tradition, the deployment of technicians will be
different. One initial problem found in this connection bears
on the definition of "tecnicos" which varies considerably from
firm to firm. In addition, it can be both a function, i.e. a
position in the firm or, the title of an occupation. We found
in our study four different situations:

(a)   positions filled by the graduates of the technical high
      schools;

(b)   positions which require secondary-level technical courses
      followed by supplementary programmes taken before starting
      activities in the firm. All enterprises interviewed have
      agreements with the technical schools by which the best
      students are recruited as they graduate. They immediately
      follow the course offered by the firms;

(c)   cases in which secondary training is only a basic pre-
      requisite with full exercise of tasks requiring a heavy
      training programme given usually after the trainee has been
      admitted to an enterprise;

(d) finally there are positions filled only by college graduates.
In most cases these are posts for engineers or lawyers.

It is difficult to know the exact number of "tecnicos" in
the enterprises surveyed due to the complex nomenclatures utilised.
Many positions described as technical have a purely administrative
character.   When we examined in detail its workforce, we observed
that, for example, enterprise B of European origin, uses almost
ten-times more medium-level technicians than enterprise A, of
American origin, and this despite the fact that both are of
similar size and use similar technology.   Another noticeable
difference is that enterprises B and C send abroad for training a
greater number of technicians than enterprise A.   All three
enterprises have their own training programme for their "tecnico"
cadres.   In general, these are hired from technical schools or
universities and they go through not only an additional training
in the enterprise school but also on-the-job training in the
operational areas (as in enterprises B and C).

The European and Japanese enterprises in our sample display
a much greater willingness to use "tecnicos" in their cadres.
These differences can only be attributed to cultural factors
because these firms face the same labour market conditions.
Nevertheless, they behave differently in their training and work
organisation.   Thus tradition more than objective data of the
Brazilian economy seem to explain the behavioural differences.

Management training programmes

The most conspicuous differences between the multinational
and the Brazilian enterprises appear in the patterns of management training.   While the domestic firms resort to a wide
variety of schemes for improvement of its staff, the multinationals systematically utilise headquarters experience.
Managers are sent very frequently indeed to headquarters for
different training programmes.

Multinationals are not taking the place of universities or
graduate schools of business.   On the contrary, they are avid
consumers of MBA graduates.   Their effort is mostly to supplement
this education in a manner quite reminiscent of what they do at
skilled-worker level.   In order to accomplish that they use headquarters expertise, methods, materials and, very often, send the
trainees there.

We could observe that the multinational enterprises tend to
have their own administrative traditions adhering to procedures
and practices developed at headquarters.   These are transmitted
via courses and teaching materials.   Some materials are translated and adapted for large-scale utilisation.   Depending on the
level of the trainees and type of programme, some materials are
used also in the original language.

The European enterprise of the sample sends a considerable
number of managers to headquarters every year.   But the Japanese
enterprise surveyed, in fact, has an even more important programme at headquarters.   It has special headquarters training
not only for management functions but also at the engineering
level.   The technicians participating in these courses are to
assimilate better techniques and know-how which they will transmit

later to their domestic staff.   In this connection handbooks
are prepared to help diffuse these new techniques ranging from
the administrative to the operational levels.

     The Brazilian enterprises surveyed resort to a broader
range of training schemes.   In the country several organisations
specialising in management development courses exist.   These
institutions operate also inside the individual Brazilian enterprises where they offer programmes tailored to the firms' requirements.

     Although none of the firms stated that management training
is their key priority, we could observe that both the multinational and the domestic enterprises spend considerable amounts
in this area, as compared to expenditures in other areas for
which they have identified bottlenecks and difficulties.

Costs and benefits of training

     According to the conventional theories, firms investing in
training expect a return later through salaries which are lower
than marginal productivity.   That is, the firm is willing to
pay for "specific" training, meaning a training that is of no
use to anybody else, otherwise they would have to pay market
wages to retain the trainees.   In all other cases, the worker
would have to pay, usually in the form of lower salaries during
the training period.   In other words, either the employee or
someone else would pay for his training.

     To understand how training is financed one must start with
the institutional and fiscal constraints.   In Brazil industrial
enterprises having over 100 employees are subject by law to a
1 per cent contribution of their payroll to SENAI and the tax
climbs to 1.2 per cent in the case of enterprises with more than
500 employees.   On the other hand, direct costs of education
and training can be rebated up to a limit of 80 per cent of this
tax revenue through an agreement between SENAI and the enterprise.
The rebate on the 1 per cent tax for all industries must be used
for training of skilled workers or "tecnicos" (middle level).
The rebate on the additional 0.2 per cent in the case of larger
firms may be used for training of higher level technical personnel
and research in the area of personnel development.   All the
surveyed enterprises have used such tax rebate agreements with
SENAI and allot these to their own courses.

     Research efforts to find out who ultimately pays for the pay-
roll tax have met with insurmountable difficulties.   It seems
impossible to tell whether the system reacts by increasing prices,
reducing wages or profits.   The question of who benefits from
training is somewhat clearer.   The relatively high job and
occupational turnover of skilled workers and managerial staff
suggests an acceptable degree of competitiveness in the market.
Firms cannot retain for too long employees who earn substantially
less than their peers in other firms.

     The new governmental Decree No. 6297 of October 1975 on
fiscal incentives allows enterprises to deduct from taxable
profits twice the amount of verified expenses on training projects.   This Act stimulated enterprises greatly to create or

expand their internal training departments (see, for example,
table 1). However, the effect of the new income tax rebate Act
has never been properly analysed. In fact, there is only now
enough accumulated evidence to warrant an evaluation.

It would be interesting though to know whether total spending
on training will increase. Big firms spend proportionately more
on training and may respond differently through smaller firms
which, from what we gather, never spend beyond the legally required
amount.

The multinational enterprises surveyed claim they prefer the
new decree because often they need personnel with a higher level
of training than that provided by SENAI (as in the case of management training). They find that with this new fiscal incentive
it enables them to offer a greater diversification of programmes.
At the same time the enterprises appreciated the contribution of
SENAI to the training of highly skilled workers. For some enterprises, like enterprise A, the Decree No. 6297 was said to be a
"lemon" because now they have first to spend to be reimbursed
later in the form of a tax deduction. Some enterprises also
complain that an excessive lead time is required for the approval
of training programmes by the Labour Ministry.

This leaves us still with the question of why enterprises
are readily spending more on training than they are forced to do
by law. The sample enterprises spend more on training than what
is warranted to take advantage of tax incentives (as indicated by
the data on total training expenditures).

The public enterprises surveyed offer training of all types
with great generosity and at all stages in the employees career.
"Public spirit" is a naive but not necessarily absurd explanation
for this. At moments we had the impression that the decision to
earmark funds for training is taken on a higher administrative
level and bears no relationship to an evaluation of concrete training needs. Higher management "thinks that training is a good
investment". Training offices therefore see themselves as spending a certain lump-sum on training rather than responding to a
participant demand for training at a given time.

As mentioned before, prodigality has sometimes created problems of excess of training especially in the white-collar area.
In the case of the multinational enterprises they seem to wish to
face their most urgent labour problem, i.e. the shortage of
workers with the required qualifications with training. Hence,
they offer "general" training for the positions or occupations
which are critical for the enterprises' performance.

In conclusion, may we suggest some explanations for the
behaviour of multinational and national enterprises with regard
to training. Let us first acknowledge the obvious and inevitable
shortage of skilled manual workers in the manufacturing sector which
has been growing considerably above 10 per cent per annum for over
two decades. Bidding on workers of other firms meets with obvious
limitations after a while. Training on the job is too slow.
Hence, enterprises may find that engagement in formal,more general
training is still profitable. It is known that big firms have
gentlemen's agreements on wage scales for each type of occupation
which means that they need not worry about losing trained labour

to other enterprises.   From a different perspective, it must
be added that labour mobility **is some**what sluggish.   Workers
do not respond instantly or inevitably to a higher wage offer
elsewhere.   Some may be reluctant to move, even if they could
obtain considerably higher wages in another enterprise;   others
do not do so immediately.   In other words, firms recuperate
their training costs on the average of their trainees rather
than on every individual case.

In this situation, it is not surprising to often find in
the enterprises we surveyed, and in particular the MNEs, the
opinion that training and training expenses will still increase
in the future.

Table 1. Enterprise A: Industrial
          relations - education
          and training -
          Synopsis

Courses given in 1978 to date (in and out of Government Convenium Law 6297 - December 1975)			Training programme for 1979 (Government Convenium Law 6297 - December 1975)		
47 courses	) Training (ind.) relations)) Special trng.) (commercial)	43 4	33 courses	) Training (ind.) relations)) Special trng.) (commercial)	28 5
43 courses	) Participants) Classes (total)) Total hours	486 47 7 409	28 courses	) Participants) Classes (total)) Total hours	570 43 5 844
4 courses	) Participants) Classes (total)) Total hours	131 13 176	5 courses	) Participants) Classes (total)) Total hours	145 7 206

A CASE STUDY FROM INDIA ON TRÁINING POLICIES OF
SELECTED MULTINATIONALS AND THEIR ROLE IN
DEVELOPMENTAL TRAINING

by

Prof. Nitisch R. De[1]

Training as human resource development

The training practices of multinational enterprises in a
developing country such as India are potentially a source of
human resource development.   This term links training and development as the way to better the quality of life of workers.   Human
resource development has both micro-economic and macro-economic
perspectives.   In the micro view, the enterprise itself is concerned with recruiting workers who have certain skills and knowledge.   The host country in which the MNE operates can have an
adequate or an inadequate supply of manpower based on this criteria.
Of course, if the people available to the enterprise already possess
the knowledge and skills necessary to be efficient workers, no
additional training is needed.   If, however, the indigenous workforce is not at the level required by the MNE, the enterprise has
three possibilities: importing workers from abroad; training
workers in the enterprise itself; and patronising existing training institutions.   To the host country, in contrast, human resource
development has a macro dimension.   The training which workers
receive because of the sophisticated needs of the MNEs can further
the country's development goals and the career objectives of the
individual worker.

This study is an examination of the human resource development
of selected MNEs in India.   The extent to which these enterprises
have contributed to development is judged on the basis of four
questions:

1.   What is the contribution of the older establishments
      (pre-1960s) to the evolution of developmental training?

2.   How different is the focus of the training engaged in
      by the more recently established MNEs?

3.   What is the relationship between the enterprise's
      organisational culture and its training policies, and
      the State's training and educational facilities?

4.   What is the future of training by MNEs in India?

For the purpose of this study the plants of four multinationals
have been selected near Delhi but which are under the direction of
Indian head offices in Bombay or Calcutta.   Information on training
in this sample of enterprises is presented against the background of
a description of conditions related to it such as: the nature of
the MNEs products and manufacturing process; the social origins of
their staff; their systems of remuneration and fringe benefits,
unionisation, etc.   In this context the potential contribution of
MNEs and their training efforts in a developing country are outlined
as are broader training and developmental goals.

---

[1] Director, Public Enterprise Centre for Continuing Education,
New Delhi.

Profiles of the enterprises studied

India being a large country with around 400 MNEs operating in trading and manufacturing on both a large and small scale, it was decided for the purpose of the case study that a comparatively underdeveloped area would be selected and that companies operating in that area would be studied. Accordingly, an area 300 to 350 kms. south-east of Delhi was selected. The general educational and training facilities existing in the two States in which the selected multinationals are established is summarised in the following table in comparison with the rest of India.

Table 1. Number of training and education facilities[1]

	State X^2	State Y^2	All India: Total
1. Universities and similar national institutions	2	18	117
2. Engineering colleges	1	14	146
3. Higher management education institutes	-	4	30
4. Polytechnics (engineering diploma-awarding institutes)	2	45	303
5. Industrial training institutes (ITI) (trade training centres)	7	50	466

[1] Institutes offering professional accounting courses are not included here.

[2] State X and State Y are states in which the MNEs included in the case study are located.

Subsidiaries of six manufacturing MNEs are located in this area. Two of them, however, could not be studied as they were having, during the relevant period (May/June 1979), industrial relations problems which made it impossible for management to participate in the study. A third company did not agree to the study being conducted in the unit located in the area in question. Although currently operating reasonably satisfactorily it has had certain ups and downs in its activities in the past. Accordingly, this company suggested that another unit located towards the north-west of Delhi in an underdeveloped region be studied, which was done. Thus, altogether we studied four production units of different MNEs operating in India. During the years of their incorporation in India, the two major commercial and industrial centres in the country were Calcutta and Bombay. It is thus understandable that the registered offices of three enterprises were originally located in Calcutta and one in Bombay. In recent years, however, the corporate head office of one enterprise has shifted to Bombay and, as such, two corporate head offices are now in Calcutta and two in Bombay.

- 89 -

The four enterprises in question come within the purview of
monopolies and restrictive trade-practice provisions of the
Government's legislation and their shareholdings are governed,
apart from other controls, by the provisions of the Foreign Exchange
Regulations Act.   While some of their manufacturing activities fall
within the ambit of the "core" sector, the bulk do not.   As such
the foreign shareholdings, by and large, are required to be restricted to 40 per cent.[1] Two of the companies have not yet complied
with this provision as required by government regulations.

We shall study the four selected units in two parts: those
which were set up before 1960 and those which were established thereafter.   This distinction will help us to understand the patterns of
human resource development in the "older" and in the "newer" locations, their similarities and their differences.

Table 2.   Profile of the sample enterprises

Parent enterprise	Total number of employees	Year of incorporation of the enter- prise in India	Subsidiary unit studied	Total number of employees	Year of setting up the units studied
A	9 000	1912	(a)	503	1967
B	10 000	1933	(b)	275	1975
C	10 000	1934	(c)	998	1958
D	5 830	1935	(d)	207	1942

Training and development

Description of units established
prior to 1960

The reason why we have distinguished the period up to 1960
from 1961 onwards is that India's accelerated industrialisation
process started in the latter phase of the second Five-Year Plan
(1955-60).   That is the period when, based on an existing foundation of industrial infrastructure, a wide range of manufacturing
activities started operations both in the developed as well as
underdeveloped regions of the country.   In our sample units (c) and
(d) belong to the first category.

---

[1] The Foreign Exchange Regulations Act of 1973 (FERA) stipulates
that in areas in which foreign investment is permitted it should be
restricted to 40 per cent of the equity capital.   However, equity
participation can be considered for industries which require highly
sophisticated technology or which are largely export-oriented.   In
the case of priority industries which require sophisticated technology but cater largely to the domestic market foreign equity investments may be allowed up to 74 per cent while in the case of industries
which are entirely for export, foreign equity even up to 100 per cent
may be permitted.   See Usha Dar: The Effects of Multinational Enterprises on Employment in India, Multinational Enterprises Programme,
Working Paper No. 9, Geneva, ILO, 1979, pp. 5 ff.

Enterprise C

This enterprise is a subsidiary of a large MNE with headquarters in the United States. It started in 1905 as an import
company selling products from the home country. In 1934, it was
incorporated as a company registered in India. It now produces
mass consumption goods in India including many destined for high
and middle-income groups although currently the rural middle class
constitutes a substantial market. The enterprise has recently
expanded its production to include a major export-oriented food
item. It also has diverse but inter-related production lines in
the chemical and agro-industrial activities. The enterprise enjoys
an image as one which is professionally managed with a strong
orientation towards product improvement, quality control, industrial
engineering techniques and adopt the profit centre concept. Some
of the senior managers of the enterprise have made a mark in other
overseas companies of the group while some have opted to head other
corporations - public and private. The enterprise has two major
R and D centres in India, one of which is considered as one of the
best in the whole enterprise group, including the R and D centres in
the United States.

The Indian subsidiary has been influenced by the management
development activities in the parent company. In the 1960s the
United States corporation went for a major organisation development
(OD) programme which received considerable attention in the world of
management, especially in management education. At that time the
corporate training division in India received encouragement to set
up a staff college to impart management education to managerial and,
to some extent, supervisory cadres. The company's recruitment to
the management cadre has been from the ranks of professional engineers, accountants and management graduates with preference given to
those Indians educated and trained in the USA. In addition to on-
the-job technical training through rigorous apprenticeships, industrial engineering techniques, value engineering and cost-control
methods have also received considerable attention.

After about a five-year period, the initial enthusiasm for OD
suffered an eclipse in the United States-based part of the enterprise and this too was reflected in the Indian subsidiary. The
corporation was then facing industrial relations problems practically
in all its major manufacturing units in an eastern state and, as such,
business suffered both in terms of production and sales. Cost control and the profit-centre concept received priority attention at that
time. The training college was closed. Training activities suffered a setback except that specific job-related training for the
technological staff continued with greater emphasis for high growth
potential staff identified through a rigorous appraisal system
modelled after the US pattern. One element in the training activity
in the enterprise is that, irrespective of the educational background
a staff member can be rotated among different jobs unless the job
demands specific technical competence. One such example is that
many bright industrial engineers over a period were promoted to
senior management positions which is often not the case in both
Indian companies and in foreign MNEs operating in India. Recruitment at this level is through open advertisement and rigorous selection mechanisms.

In the late 1970s after the Indianisation of top management
positions, management development has been revived. A senior level
training manager has been appointed who is seeking to establish

training activities on a planned basis.   In 1979-80, eight high-
level management development programmes were undertaken for senior
to near-top level managers.   Simultaneously, management trainees
were put through rigorous programmes in the corporate office as
well as in the production centres.   Training of the sales staff
is also not neglected.   R and D staff are exposed to the developments in various group companies in India and abroad.   The enterprise also appointed a US consulting firm to study and recommend
action to improve managerial culture and effectiveness.   Although
modelled after the US management practices, in recent years the
enterprise has adapted itself well to the Indian pattern in that a
perquisite system has been introduced for the first time in the
enterprise.   The practice before the change was that the managerial
cadre was entitled to a gross salary but not to any other recurring
benefits.   The enterprise discovered that because of housing and
transport problems in the major industrial centres it was necessary
to pay subsidies for these expenses to the managerial employees if
it wanted to retain them.

Unit (c)

This unit located just outside the capital city of the State
is one of the major manufacturing centres.   It is the only factory
in the enterprise system to make a mass production item under
different brand names.   The enterprise's products are popular
because of their quality and aesthetic design.   The technology
involves chemical processing activities resulting in the products
being assembled through conveyor chain, packaged and despatched.
The number of operations involved exceed those in units (a) and (b).
The unit employs 998 employees and is thus the largest unit included
in our case study.   Capital investment in the plant has been in the
nature of Rs.70 million.

The unit is responsible for training and development activities
for the non-managerial cadre although the activities are essentially
confined to the supervisory personnel who are mostly science graduates or diploma holders in different disciplines of engineering.
Generally, supervisors can get promotion to higher levels provided
they have the requisite educational qualifications along with a
consistent record of high performance.

The activities of the unit have been organised on a layout
system planned by industrial engineers; and the production target,
which is around 7.5 million units a year, is co-ordinated at the
production centre under the production planning and control department.   Workers are mostly semi-skilled and with regard to recruitment, government employment exchanges are usually notified.
Historically, unskilled labour has been recruited and trained on
the job.   Only in recent years have the Indian ITI (Industrial
Training Institute) trade-trained workers been employed primarily
for tool-room and maintenance activities.

All jobs are elaborately described and the supervisory to
higher-level grades are evaluated against what is known as MOPS
(measurement of performance).   This is done quarterly.   Below the
departmental head level the reviews are conducted every month.

There has been no recruitment in the unit since 1973 except in
the category of management staff.   A production incentive scheme
is a major motivation to workmen and the index of productivity rise

is reflected in the fact that eight units were produced in 1978 per
man-hour as compared to 5.5 units in 1975. On an average, the
incentive earning of a direct hourly-rated worker is Rs.120 per
month.

Supervisors do participate in supervisory training programmes
organised internally as well as externally. These programmes are
particularly oriented towards safety methods, production planning
and control, cost accountancy, statistical quality control and
report writing. Since 1973, about four programmes were held in
the unit on production planning and control, and on effective communication organised by the National Institute of Training in
Industrial Engineering (NITIE). The unit also engages a number
of summer vacation trainees from engineering colleges and management
schools located in the State. This is more need-based than a
regular yearly programme. So far such trainees have been utilised
for market survey activities.

There has been a consistent effort to upgrade the technology
by improving productivity and reducing cost. In 1973-74 there
were 1,100 employees which have now come down to 998. This has
been possible by offering attractive retirement terms to the
employees.

Enterprise D

This enterprise is a subsidiary of a British MNE. It started
its operations in India in 1935. It is the only one in the sample
which produces mainly products for industrial use. In addition, the
MNE manufactures a small number of other items for health care.

The enterprise enjoys a large share of the market. Some of
its products are high-technology oriented. The enterprise has been
known in India as technologically sound, stable and somewhat con-
servative in its management style. Along with a large managerial
cadre it has also a small but strong cadre of competent professional
accountants. Manufacturing facilities apart, marketing is a major
task of the company, particularly in view of increasing competition
even though no other Indian competitors come anywhere near the scale
of operation of enterprise D. Keeping in tune with the emphasis on
management training and development in the parent company in the
United Kingdom, this enterprise set up for the first time a management development division in the Indian head office in 1967. That
was the year when a consultant from the UK studied the need for
management development activities in the enterprise and a series of
steps were initiated to this end at the corporate level. In recent
years several Indian consultants have been associated with this
division's activities.

Training activities essentially emanate from the performance
appraisal system for the career personnel, i.e. management staff.
It not only measures and analyses the performance of a manager
against set tasks and targets but also identifies his areas of
strength and weaknesses resulting in the creation of an inventory
of training needs. There is a training budget approved every year
by the board. In recent years the training division has also added
to its responsibility by taking up planned training for the supervisory cadre. It seems that this is the only enterprise in our
sample which has a regular schedule of activities for training supervisors.

Management training is composed of a company orientation programme, a human relations programme, a tailor-made two-week programme for the "high fliers" and also certain specific programmes such as management of conflict, personal growth through transactional analysis, management of innovation and production and planning-related technical courses. The training division in the corporate office is adequately staffed and it reports to the chief executive of personnel. Supervisory training programmes are centrally planned on the basis of needs expressed by production and marketing units but implemented in a decentralised fashion in the industrial production units. These programmes essentially deal with industrial engineering techniques, industrial relations, safety measures, cost control and human relations.

Attempts were also made by enterprise D to develop a cadre of trainers for training in various units but this has not worked out satisfactorily. R and D activities can be conceived as a part of developmental programmes and for that a separate company has been formed in which the enterprise holds 26 per cent of the invested capital. Enterprise D also runs technical programmes for its associated companies in some of the neighbouring countries.

While in the initial years recruitment to the management cadre attracted Indians educated in the UK, the present trend is to employ India-trained engineers and accountants through open market recruitment.

Unit (d)

Unit (d) set up in 1942 and employing 207 persons is located in the heart of an old industrial centre. The industrial centre was known for defence ordinance factories and later for the textile industry. This unit manufactures products which have wide industrial uses in manufacturing plants. The reason for choosing this location during the war years was the concentration of other industries in this city as well as the communication facility that it offered for the transport of its products. Most of the employees are unskilled and semi-skilled.

Unit (d) is one of the smallest production centres of enterprise D. There are 100 workers directly engaged on the shop floor and about the same number of clerical, sales and other staff. There are six managers.

In the initial years recruitment was mostly based on personal knowledge of the applicant and recommendations. Managers and key supervisors were brought in from other locations. These managers and supervisors offered jobs to candidates located through various contacts. There were many cases where persons in the household employment of these key personnel of unit (d) were recruited. Caste consideration in recruitment was not altogether unknown. Naturally, there had been large numbers of employees who were illiterates, mostly engaged in unskilled work. In the first few years there were 50 employees which have gradually risen to the current level of 207. In 1977, there were 14 vacancies in the workman cadre which was the last year of recruitment by the unit.

What is stated about the method of recruitment of workers
is applicable to the clerical cadre also.   This has created
some problems in recent years as the complexity of office work
has increased.   A large number of returns and statistics have
to be regularly transmitted to the corporate office and also to
different government agencies.   Account systems have become
more complicated.   Older semi-literate clerical employees now
find it difficult to adjust to this qualitative change in work
demands.

Unit (d) does not undertake any formal training activity,
there is a provision for on-the-job training which can result in
an unskilled worker becoming a semi-skilled one and in upgrading
the skill levels of clerks.   Since unit (d) is an old unit, a
substantial number of persons who joined the office or the shop
floor have, over the years, been able to rise to higher levels
depending on the unit's growth and vacancies.   However, from the
1960s onwards, efforts have been made to ensure that the aspiring
employees acquire educational qualifications for promotion.   The
state education system with provisions for evening classes and
correspondence courses has somewhat helped the employees in
acquiring higher general skills.   There are, however, no company-
promoted incentives schemes which could induce employees to follow
such courses.

Apart from on-the-job training, as mentioned, there is another
widespread practice of offering acting assignments to employees
when a senior employee is absent on leave.   While this is not
"training" in the full sense of the word it is an occasion for
career advancement.   An employee is observed in his "acting" job,
which is taken into account at the time of promotion.   Generally,
an unskilled worker gets two promotions in the course of his
career, as do the clerical employees.   From the 1960s onward, all
vacancies have been notified to the government employment exchange.

Trade union leaders are more concerned, as the interviews
reveal, with major terms and conditions of employment such as the
wage scale, working conditions, fringe benefits and so on rather
than with training practices of the unit.   They do not show much
concern for and interest in training and development activities
for their members which may be a matter of priorities more than
one of neglect of the area.

As in the case of enterprise C and unit (c), and in enterprise D as well as in unit (d), there is no planned development
through training of the workman category.   The Government sponsors
a workers' education programme at several training centres in
industrial areas.   The programme trains workers who, in turn, are
expected to hold classes for their colleagues in the factory,
subject to the management's approval.   This scheme is essentially
meant to provide a modicum of knowledge of various industrial laws
and regulations that govern factory workers as well as those
employed in mining operations and plantations.

These units periodically patronise this programme by assigning
workers to the government training centre.   There is, however, no
follow-up scheme.   Workers' career planning is essentially determined by the experience they gather on the job and by the combined
criteria of seniority and merit by which they are upgraded to a
higher category.   Promotion is vacancy-based.   Similarly, there

is no developmental programme for the clerical employees except
that some ambitious clerks, on their own initiative, train themselves through correspondence courses to acquire professional
skills and knowledge in accountancy.

Description of units established
after 1960

Enterprise A

This enterprise was originally a British company operating
in India. Over the years, it became a public limited company
with minority shareholders in the United Kingdom. It had practically a monopoly position initially in one product range after
which a second product was introduced. A third product, entirely
export-oriented will soon be manufactured. The products are mass
consumption items - in all price ranges. The enterprise still
occupies the upper-most position in the Indian market, although
there are two other British MNEs operating in the field. In
fact, enterprise A is associated with a few sister companies under
the umbrella of the British principal, although they operate
independently in India.

Initially, the company's recruitment programme was confined
to employing public school-educated young men from the high-middle
to higher strata of urban income groups. They constituted the
bulk of the marketing cadre. Training has been essentially on
the job and the in-company formal training on marketing and sales-
manship used to be handled by the higher echelon of expatriate
executives.

Around 1960 emphasis shifted from the original recruitment
pattern to management trainees either with a business school or a
social science background. With the introduction of manufacturing
activities located primarily in five centres of India, induction of
engineering graduates and undergraduates (diploma holders) has been
initiated. A special feature of the newer manufacturing units is
that these are located a moderate distance from a city or town on
the assumption that the working-class culture of urban centres
ought not to influence the newly set-up factories.

Management development as a corporate function has been of
recent origin (late 1960s). Because of the diverse marketing
activities, the company's initial management programmes have been
built around the theme of effective communication. In the early
years the emphasis was on the managerial personnel's ability to
provide leadership to their subordinates, but gradually the
emphasis has shifted to cost management in relation to production,
maintenance, technology improvement and some modicum of R and D.
Industrial engineering plays a major role in work rationalisation
because most of the consumer products of the enterprise are meant
for the poorer sections of the population and, as such, price has
to be kept within limits. In recent years, emphasis has shifted
to the recruitment of qualified accountants.

There has been manpower and career planning as an on-going
exercise for the past three years. Placement and personnel transfers are planned accordingly. Formal in-company management
programmes are few and far between. Occasionally technique-
oriented need-based workshops are held under a centralised plan.

Recently, a personnel policy handbook was prepared for a new factory which was being set up for a third product line of a food item entirely meant for export. It is a highly mechanised plant and the packaging processes are such that blind persons can be employed. On the whole, it may be mentioned that the company's recruitment, training and developmental strategy is marked by the following features:

(a) emphasis on urbanised, articulate young cadre of management trainees to man ultimately the senior positions in the company in marketing, production, engineering and finance disciplines. Their training is primarily internal and functional. They do, however, progress in the enterprise on the strength of their achievements, indicating they can occupy in the future senior managerial positions. They have essentially a corporate function;

(b) in so far as the factory operations are concerned, the supervisory and clerical cadres are generally expected to remain in that cadre throughout their career. Only the exceptional ones could cross the barrier and join management ranks. A particular feature of this policy will be mentioned when we shall discuss unit (a);

(c) worker recruitment is primarily confined to local labour from the nearby villages. This considerably reduces the need for such social overheads as a housing colony. Except for the maintenance jobs all other workers are recruited as unskilled workmen and trained on the job to become semi-skilled.

While management development as a concept and practice is confined to the management cadre, almost next to nothing has been done or even planned for the worker level. For the supervisory cadre some knowledge and skill-oriented seminars are organised in particular related to problems of shop-floor discipline and productivity.

Unit (a)

This unit employs 503 persons most of whom are unskilled and semi-skilled labour. It is located at a place which is one hour by road from the nearest town. The primary advantage of setting-up this unit in 1967 was its rail transport connection. The goods are handled in bulk and it was felt that apart from acting as a process unit for its main product, the unit can also act as a main storage centre for the products which could move to northern and western India, including the local market. The current capital valuation of unit (a) is about Rs.30 million.

The operation of unit (a) is confined to mixing certain production items according to instructions given by the technical department located in the head office. For this purpose, a small conveyor system is utilised. The skill level of the workers of unit (a) is low except for the maintenance group. Older machines are gradually being replaced by new ones. There is no housing colony in this backward area which is surrounded by a large number of villages. The nearest "civilised" spot is the railway establishment. Workers come from nearby areas and those who belong to the supervisory cadre have rented houses. The managers live in the nearby town.

In 1967 when the factory was set up, its recruitment was at the factory gate. Local people turned up; there was no minimum qualification requisite and, in fact, most of these persons were illiterate. They were subjected to a full medical check-up, and originally 150 workers were taken on as casual employees. They were observed on the job according to such criteria as ability to learn, ability to cultivate discipline, over-all conduct in the factory and reputation in the vicinity. After a trial period of six months, 80 persons were recruited. During this period they were subjected to monthly appraisal by the departmental heads. Later on, as the modernisation process started, it was necessary to recruit semi-skilled workers par-ticularly for maintenance jobs. In this context, the Industrial Training Institute (ITI) trainees were recruited. For the first time, literate employees were inducted in the workman category. In recent years there has been no recruitment in this category.

With regard to the recruitment of the supervisory cadre, the local employment exchange is notified and the positions are also advertised. Educational qualifications up to the level of a first degree are desirable except for those who hold a diploma in mechanical or electrical engineering. In addition to inter-views, they are subjected to written tests.

In the plant there is no training establishment. These activities are under the administrative officer who primarily handles local industrial relations problems. Industrial rela-tions issues are, however, settled on an all-India basis in so far as major and common matters are concerned. At the local level industrial relations management is confined to disputes regarding production incentive schemes, working conditions, grievances of different kinds, and so on.

There is no training plan or budget for the unit. In 1977, perhaps for the first time in the factory's history, two pro-grammes were run in the factory for the supervisory and clerical personnel to increase productivity. The course was taught by an external agency - the National Productivity Council. A similar programme was planned for 1979. Each time such a train-ing programme is planned by unit (a) it, and the cost estimated, has to be approved by headquarters.

An interesting point is that the clerical employees are interchangeable with shop-floor supervisors. The technical component of the factory work is essentially handled by the management cadre, such as shift assistants, production manager, assistant factory manager and factory engineer. The supervisor's job is essentially to ensure that the workers are on the job and properly deployed. Production norms are set for each machine and the production target is measured by packaging goods to the extent of 400 tons per week on two-shift operations. In all 433 hourly rated workmen and 29 other staff (messengers and similar employees) are controlled by 35 supervisory and clerical personnel and 8 managers.

The production incentive scheme induces personnel to learn and work through higher emoluments and allowances. Unit (a) is part of an enterprise which constitutes a high wage/salary enclave. The production incentive scheme does not cover the supervisory cadre but the allowances are liberal by Indian standards. There is an additional incentive in the form of wage incrementals depend-ing on length of service.

A visit to the factory and discussions with the managers, supervisory personnel, workers and trade union leaders indicated that the workers are satisfied with their wages and, in fact, are motivated to work efficiently at repetitive tasks due to incentives tied to productivity.

It may be observed that for the purpose of the production incentive scheme jobs are broadly categorised into class (a) and class (b) jobs.   In the event that there are, on a particular day, less of class (a) jobs because of a production change or machine hold-up, workers can be shifted to class (b) although their incentive earnings would be adversely affected.   The trade union is rather weak in this factory and management is therefore more paternalistic.   Comparative isolation from the industrial environment added to the fact that many of the workers also have agricultural activities in the nearby villages partly explains the paternalism and weak trade unions.   An industrially oriented working class has not yet emerged in unit (a) even though it has now been in existence for more than ten years.

Enterprise B

Enterprise B, a subsidiary of a Dutch-British MNE started its manufacturing and trading activities in 1933.   Like enterprise A, it has diverse operations particularly in trade throughout the country.   The manufacturing activities of enterprise B are, however, located in a limited number of sites as is the case for enterprise A.   The products of enterprise B are also mass consumption items.   However, the nature of the products is such that they cater to the needs of middle to high-income groups.

The multinational parent has worldwide operations in food, chemicals, animal feeds, washing materials and some other specific items.   Regarding management style, the Indian subsidiary is more influenced by the British partner, although especially in respect of R and D, some main contacts are held with the Dutch partner.

The numerous products of enterprise B with diverse brand varieties, are manufactured in a number of factories located in the old industrial sites as well as, in recent years, in underdeveloped Indian regions.   The marketing network of the enterprise is well organised even though sales are handled by numerous local agents and distributors.   However, the well-organised activities of the enterprise for some of its production are in direct competition with Indian small-scale and cottage industries which competively speaking are in a considerably disadvantaged position.   They do not have, in the first place, the R and D backup of the multinational enterprise nor do they enjoy its well-geared marketing network.   Only some of its activities are in the "core" sector (i.e. that in which foreign ownership is restricted to 40 per cent) and, as such, it has scope for further expansion provided it dilutes its foreign equity, a requirement with which the company has yet to comply.

The company has an established R and D facility in the same city where the corporate office is located.   Its management has a high professional standard;   the number of expatriates had gradually gone down, and at the moment, there is no expatriate manager employed by the company.   There are short visits by overseas specialists on specific projects.   On the other hand,

the Indian managerial personnel do get assignments either at
headquarters of the MNE or in its subsidiaries located in other
countries.   The company takes great pains in the recruitment of
management cadre and its selection procedure in this respect is
well designed.   Professional engineers, accountants and graduates
of management schools are preferred.   Until about 1970 it was
fashionable among the brighter students of the management schools
to be hired by this prestigious enterprise, but of late the better
students prefer to obtain positions in selected public enterprises
or to continue their education abroad.   None the less the management cadre of enterprise B from the junior to top level enjoys
the reputation of being highly professional and efficient.   Like
enterprise C, this enterprise also has deputed over the years a
number of top executives to various responsible assignments in
government and public enterprises.   The enterprise follows the
British tradition in identifying "highfliers" in the initial
period of their career and moves them up the ladder at a faster
pace.   While reviewing the management development strategy of
headquarters, Douglas McGregor, the famous specialist in industrial
organisation, was somewhat critical of what he called "the crown-
prince approach" of the corporation.   Nevertheless, this culture
persists.

       At the corporate level, the personnel and training functions
are directly under the responsibility of a senior member of the
board.   While personnel functions are undertaken in close collaboration with the training division, they are primarily concerned
with long-range manpower planning based on strict industrial
engineering norms, detailed job description and identification of
"responsibility centres".   Career planning for the executives is
based on periodical evaluation of performance, and these exercises
and activities are dovetailed with management development plans
prepared by the training group.   Management of industrial relations is handled with some emphasis on the legal aspects.   This
is indicative of the lack of active interest in developmental
training of the workman category, a phenomenon which we have
observed in all other cases.   Training for supervisors is
essentially decentralised and, as in most other cases, less
imaginative and weakly conceived and executed.

Unit (b)

       This unit is located near an old town.   When it was set up
in 1975, this was the first time that an industrial organisation
had been established there.   Unit (b) makes one product under
two brand names, both highly sophisticated.   The chemical processing is of superior technology.   The unit employs 275 persons
and the average age of the workforce is 22 years.   Packaging is
the major activity in which most of the employees are engaged (as
in unit (a)).   The Employees are essentially unskilled and semi-
skilled although deliberate attempts are being made to make the
employees somewhat multi-skilled in inter-related activities.
R and D activities are extremely limited, as in unit (a).   Its
current capital asset is placed at Rs.20 million.   The unit also
operates in the "core" sector of activities according to the
government regulation.

       It would be worthwhile to look into the motivation as to why
the unit was set up in a distant, underdeveloped place.   Under

the local government, as well as the central government schemes, the unit enjoys the following incentives and rebates for having come to this area:

1. the local government gave a subsidy of Rs.4 million for setting-up the establishment in the State;

2. 20 per cent of taxable profits are treated as tax deductible;

3. 7 1/2 per cent of the capital employed is also treated as tax deductible;

4. toll tax (entry and exit of raw materials and goods) to the amount of Rs.40 per ton will not apply to this unit for a period of 10 years;   and

5. finally, the unit also received the central government subsidy of 15 per cent of the capital investment subject to a maximum of Rs.1.5 million.

Yet another advantage, though not under the government regulation, has been that the location had no previous industrial culture.   This means that trade union activities could be expected to be conducive to the smooth operation of the plant.

The management of the project construction was done in record time by lining up reputed and trusted contractors.   Close supervision was maintained by management.   Simultaneously, selective recruitment in key categories was undertaken.   Apart from the managerial cadre which came from other units of the enterprise, recruitment was confined to the people living in the State.   At the supervisory level eight chemical engineers from the local engineering college were recruited as trainees who were exposed to on-the-job training in other locations of the enterprise.   Their progress was closely monitored.   At the end of a year-long training period, four were retained and posted in the unit.   Similarly, contacts were established with the local ITI (industrial training institute) and trade apprentices were recruited at the lowest level.   Seventy per cent of the worker category carry out unskilled jobs and through on-the-job training and experience they move up to semi-skilled jobs such as workers on the mill side and as machine operators.   Workers thus upgraded represent roughly 20 per cent of the workforce.   Ten per cent of the workforce belongs to the skilled category who are mostly in fitting, electrical, boiler attending and instrumentation jobs. Initially about 25 per cent of the skilled category were brought from outside, as these skills were not available in the state of implantation.   The local employment exchange was not consulted as the unit felt that its direct contacts with the ITI would be more fruitful.   One innovative action was taken by the unit. Having found that the ITI-trained workers were far below the expected standard, the unit management offered technical assistance to the ITI to design training programmes with particular emphasis on practical training.   This was the only instance in the units we studied where a close liaison was maintained for a number of years with a local trade school.

For the worker category extensive on-the-job training was chalked out and implemented.   The training programme was broken down into weeks and months and detailed operational programmes

were rigorously implemented.   Rudiments of scientific
education; familiarisation with process technology; exposure
to the mechanics of various machines and equipment; and
exposure to different aspects of safety, engineering practices,
discipline and related issues were emphasised.   At the end of
each module of the programme the trainees were subjected to
written, as well as practical, tests.   It is quite evident
from a detailed study carried out on the shop floor that the
recruits with rural background could acclimatise themselves
to the factory-work culture.   In fact, the training has
resulted in such an identification with the factory that the
trade union, which was formed later on, did not develop much
independence.   Management even took the initiative for having
a trade union formed ensuring at the same time that no outside
leadership was introduced.   Regular elections to the union
executive committee are held which has rendered it more independent but there is a feeling that management still wields considerable influence as evidenced by our interviews with the more
qualified employees.

On-the-job training still continues to play a dominant role
in unit (b) and a lowest cadre shop-floor employee is associated
with a higher skilled worker so that he can become an apprentice
to the senior partner. ⦁Shop-floor supervision is active and
"tight" control is maintained.   Most of the supervisors are
engineering graduates from state training institutions and they
have also undergone rigorous on-the-job training.   Unlike what
happens with the managerial cadre, who are periodically exposed
to modern management skills and techniques, the supervisory
cadre is left to learn from the superiors while on the job.
For this category, good pay still acts as a motivator and the
turnover rate is low except for highly skilled persons.   In
recent months workers from the tool room and technically experienced supervisors have left for better jobs in other companies.

Cost control is a major contribution to productivity rise.
The industrial engineering culture is strong in the enterprise
and is reflected in unit (b) as well.   There is an incentive
scheme with strict production norms and the scheme is not a
bargainable item for the trade union.   Individual disputes in
relation to the operation of the incentive scheme can, however,
be discussed.   The scheme is essentially based on time measured
by minutes, in an hour, spent on work as reflected in production.
The quality of the item produced is also taken into account.

The social overheads of the unit have been kept at the very
minimum.   There is no housing colony.   Most of the workers
being local, they stay in their own houses or in the rented
quarters in the nearby town.   There are four houses within the
factory premises for the senior managers.   Other managers have
been extended liberal housing subsidy to enable them to stay in
the best neighbourhood of the nearby town.

Another strategy adopted to maintain high productivity level
is to deploy workers on multi-skilled jobs.   This is particularly
so for maintenance staff who are to carry out multiple jobs as
their training module has been designed along these lines.   As
was earlier mentioned, unit (b) was able to reach a high level of
productivity within a span of only two years, partly because of
the discipline that has been sustained in the unit.   In 1978, an

agreement was entered into with the union.   The first clause
of the settlement reads as follows: "(a) The employees will
co-operate with the management in improving productivity;
(b) Employees will follow constitutional and peaceful means
for resolving disputes, if any, as and when they arise."

    The management has somewhat simplified its range of
activities by farming out a large number of activities to contact labour.   Maintenance of the factory and loading and
unloading operations are handled by outside contractors.   It
may be that the state Government in its eagerness to encourage
industries to come to the State, does not always enforce the
various labour statutes and regulations with vigour, including
regulations on environmental protection.

    Again, while considerable attention is paid to the develop-
ment of management cadre, very little has been done in unit (b)
for the development of the supervisory cadre in terms of preparing them to move to managerial positions in the future.   At
the time of visiting this establishment (May 1979) only one
programme for the supervisors had been organised.   It was concerned with the maintenance of shop-floor discipline.   Another
programme on the subject of productivity was scheduled to be
held in the same year.   The programmes for supervisory cadre are
therefore specific.   They do not necessarily seem to expand the
managerial horizon of the supervisory cadre.

The enterprises' organisational culture, developmental training and the educational structure

    In this section, we highlight four conclusions derived from
this case study.   First, we shall assume three parameters of
environment which affect the organisational culture of the
enterprise.   Normally, MNEs perceive only the parameter of
their business interests.   The enterprises are concerned mainly
with the consumers' choice of their products.   Except for one
enterprise in our sample, all cater to the needs of middle to
higher-income groups in the country.   In a sense, their market
is assured.   The second parameter of the environment is the
local, state and federal Government.   Government regulation in
a semi-planned economy is understandable.   The third factor
influencing the behaviour of the MNEs is the trade unions.
Efforts are made by multinationals to maintain industrial peace
through various forms of interaction with the trade unions and
fostering worker development.   It seems, however, that the wider
context of the environment does not play a large role in the
planning done by the enterprises.

    Second, it follows from our first conclusion that develop-
mental training of blue-collar and white-collar employees and,
to a great extent, of the supervisory cadre, is either absent or
visibly neglected.   The collective bargaining mechanisms for the
worker groups and with respect to supervisory cadre have resulted
in pay scales and other benefits which seem to keep the employees
concerned satisfied.   Training, therefore, does not provide job
satisfaction to the employee, which means that the growth through
training of the workforce is not a major concern.   In one unit
under the corporate training plan, supervisory training has been

accorded some recognition. In so far as the workers are
concerned, apart from on-the-job training, hardly any other
viable schemes exist. It is relevant to mention that Etzioni's
thesis on a utilitarian calculative model of organisational
authority-based stimulus which brings forth a calculative
response of commitment from the employees[1] seems to operate in
the sampled companies. The employees are mainly concerned with
monetary benefits which are offered in the form of wages and
other components in the pay packet and production incentive
earnings under rigid industrial engineering norms.

In fact the federated trade unions, under strong politically
affiliated leadership, also bargain hard for monetary benefits for
the members. They do not concern themselves much with career
planning and learning-oriented developmental issues. Upward
mobility of workmen and lower-level supervisors is conceived in
terms of the upgrading of pay scales and the pay packet, both
by management and by trade unions. In the units we have had
opportunities to meet with the local trade union leaders and
employees as well. It was the same refrain all through. Their
response to our study was uniform: "Why are you interested in
knowing about training and development? We are already trained
and we all do a good job. What more do we need? Instead, you
should study our pay and benefits which should be more because
our productivity is high and the company is making a lot of profit."

In a way, these manifestations bring up the larger issue of
organisational socialisation (Schein, 1971).[2] The goals of these
enterprises, as concretely reflected in their units under study,
are distinct and set. Profit maximisation being the primary
objective, selection of product lines, choice of technology, size
of operation, etc. are related to market segments. Following
this, the enterprises develop commensurate management mechanisms
to socialise the employees. If in the older establishments
recruitment of lower-level employees was haphazard and "unscien-
tific" this is not so in the newer establishments. But the
basic thrust has been the same. Rigorous, repetitive training
on the job under controlled supervisors who, in turn, operate
within programmed task boundaries with very limited discretionary
content in their job. The reward structure, essentially conceived in financial terms, takes care of conformism culture at
the lower levels. At the higher levels more developmental
opportunities are offered. However, no culture of "dissent" is
encouraged or sustained at this level.

It should be stressed, however, that the scenario we have
painted should not depict a negative image of the enterprises.
There are a variety of complex motivating factors in operation
which certainly exceed those highlighted by us. Even though
social interaction in the work situation is apparently restrictive
in the corporate offices of these enterprises, in the plants the

---

[1] See Amitai Etzioni: A Comparative Analysis of Complex
Organizations (New York, 1975).

[2] Edgar H. Schein: "Organizational Socialization and the
Profession of Management", in Kolb, D.A. et al, (ed.),
Organizational Psychology (New Jersey, 1971).

culture is refreshingly different.   By and large, managers,
supervisors and workers maintain informal work relations.   Many
managers mix with workers while having lunch.   Individual
grievances are promptly attended to.   Thus a sort of liberal
management style is cultivated, somewhat distinct from that of
indigenous family-run industrial complexes where the style is
patently authoritarian-cum-paternalistic.

Third, all training activities, planned or ad hoc, are geared
towards efficiency: managers are trained to be better managers.
Efficiency is also the goal of training for supervisors and lower
categories of employees.   Developmental training, the way we
have defined it in our opening statement, hardly exists.

Fourth, there is selected utilisation of training structures
created by government agencies over a period of the past two
decades.   Graduates of institutes of technology, regional
engineering colleges, institutes of management, brighter students
of the better universities and professionally trained accountants
are inducted on a planned basis at the managerial level.   By and
large, the selection pattern is such that urbanised middle to
higher-income group people figure in the recruitment programmes.
On the other hand graduates from these very same institutes, who
belong to the poorest sections of population (particularly the
backward groups and the tribals) rarely obtain employment in MNEs.
This is in sharp contrast to what the public sector has been
steadily implementing (i.e. the recruitment of trained personnel
from minority groups).   However, despite government recommendations as such, there are no directives.   The enterprises are
operating in a free market in so far as recruitment is concerned.

Similar is the case with the graduates of the industrial
training institutes.   It is only in recent years that these
enterprises, particularly for their manufacturing units, are
taking the graduates of the ITIs.   What is significant, however,
is that these enterprises' investment in the institutional infrastructure is minimal.   There are instances of a few scholarships
but no deliberate plans to support these institutes financially
or otherwise.   However, we find that one unit in our sample has
taken active interest in helping an industrial training institute
to redesign its curricula to include practical training.   In
summary, there is considerable room for greater co-operation
between the enterprises sampled and the local training institutions.

It is relevant to draw a comparison with local industrial
concerns and public enterprises.   The picture at the national
and state level can be tentatively described as follows:

(a)   at the professional levels, the multinationals seek to
      recruit the brighter graduates from the professional training
      institutions.   Even though connections with and recommenda-
      tions from influential persons are at times accommodated,
      quality is not sacrificed.   In other private enterprises,
      there is wide variation.   Some are quality conscious; the
      majority, however, is less so.   Perhaps their experience is
      that the brighter young recruits often do not remain with
      the enterprise.   Organisational traditionalism often stands
      in the way of the adjustment of such young people.   There
      are often caste and regional considerations in recruitment.
      Loyalty being an important factor, such considerations are
      seen as conducive to identification with the employers.

In public enterprises (federal sector), because of their complex technology, attempts are also made to recruit higher calibre candidates. However, these corporations do recruit sizeable numbers every year, by necessity, resulting in the recruitment of mediocre staff as well.

What is, however, common in all these enterprises is a lack of an active interest in the induction of women employees at professional levels, except in the medical set-up;

(b) in the matter of supervisory selection, the multinationals seek to keep the intake to a minimum, therefore they can look for quality. In other cases, mediocrity is often found. However, in public enterprises a significant section of supervisory personnel come from the ranks. They are promoted but often not trained for the new responsibilities. The number of these people is also large in the larger corporations;

(c) in respect of the workman category, the multinationals particularly take care not to recruit what they refer to as "over-qualified" workers. They prefer to recruit (except for skilled and semi-skilled jobs) inexperienced labour from the vicinity in which they are located. Local private enterprises follow the same pattern. The public enterprises, at least the older ones, undertook a massive recruitment of untrained workers from the vicinity, including displaced persons whose land had been acquired for establishing the industrial complexes. Over the past one-and-a-half decades, the recruitment system has changed and the bulk of the intake is from ITIs. These industrial training institute candidates must undergo selection tests;

(d) the most significant change can be observed with respect to recruitment of members of the (socio-economically) disadvantaged population. Here, the public enterprises are the most active. Their investment in the post-recruitment training for employees from these population groups is considerable in terms of time and money.

Naturally, the public enterprises maintain closer liaison with the educational infrastructure created by the state agencies. There are instances where some of these enterprises help to design special programmes for their own technical personnel trained in these institutes. In this context the enterprises offer substantial financial and technical support. Encouragement is also provided for the teaching and research staff of these public institutes to undertake applied research in the enterprises to acquire knowledge and research capability.

On the whole, it can be observed that in the case of the multinational enterprises a tendency to render less service to the environment in human resource development as compared to securing from it their specific manpower requirements is shown. This may be connected with the industrial engineering culture prevading in these enterprises which has resulted in an efficiency-proneness of various forms. This is not necessarily an undesirable element by itself. At the same time, it reflects a sustained

culture of "economism".   The mediating role between an employee
and work is relegated to money and other emoluments offered that
are convertible in monetary terms.   The "social use value" of
the fruits of their labour is pushed into the background.
Professionalisation, of which MNEs are justifiably proud, seems
to have a major component of economic calculus, rather than social
calculus, the importance of which is no less significant in an
underdeveloped country such as India;   it is clearly more important
than in the consumption-oriented richer countries.

One last point is the feeling of two segments of India's
population towards MNE training.   These **can** be summed up in the
following manner:

(a)   among the government functionaries divergent views prevail.
      However, there is a general feeling that the MNEs are
      managed, professionally, with competence.   There is an
      implied feeling that this style of management should be
      emulated in other sectors of industrial and commercial
      operations.

      Specifically, regarding training and development
      activities, the views differ much more.   Some people
      believe that the multinationals can assure work from their
      employees through effectively managing financial incentives
      in various forms.   Others believe that they tend to gene-
      rate an "enclave culture" of "economism" and foster a kind
      of lifestyle which is not conducive to development.   They
      also point out that workers and supervisors are not treated
      as human resources to be elevated to the level of
      development that a productive system is capable of;

(b)   the members of the educational infrastructure are more
      critical in their expressions.   The criticisms are on two
      counts: one, that the MNEs give undue importance to pro-
      fessionally trained students who express themselves well
      in English and are smart and "modernised" in their general
      bearing.   These students represent a particular socio-
      economic strata.   Students who are equally knowledgeable
      and perhaps more serious but less "modernised" (which does
      not necessarily mean that they have less vitality) are left
      out.   Second, their support of the Indian training infra-
      structure is considered a function of what they are able
      to do in view of their resources to help to develop the
      local institutions.

      One exception to this stance is the centrally run
      institutes of management included in our survey.   By and
      large the faculty members of the institutes believe that
      the MNEs provide special encouragement by engaging them in
      consulting assignments.   This helps them greatly to test
      a conceptual framework in concrete situations.

Outlook

As a final consideration we wish to address four issues with
an eye on the future role in a country such as India.   First of
all, the MNEs in our sample can be described as technocratic
organisations (as distinct from bureaucratic ones).   These
organisations work on the premise of technocratic ethos. Thus,

rules, regulations, procedural systems and subordination of
specific goals to fixed limits set by the complexity of checks
and balances resulting in a form of organisation involution are
fortunately absent in the MNEs. This is, however, not to imply
that they do not have their operating manuals, including
accounting systems and procedures.

Organisation goals defined in concrete tasks and targets -
physical as well as financial - are the major motivating forces
for the ongoing activities in the enterprises. Getting ahead
with the job and recalling the need for cost effectiveness in
respect of inputs, processing and outputs, commensurate with
concern for quality to maximise profits have made these organisations open to improvements in whatever way these are achievable.
Concern for updated techniques whether in production or marketing
remains a prime objective. These are some characteristics of
technocratic culture. Its relevance to an underdeveloped
country is unquestionable. Productive organisations in all
countries reflect this capitalist and socialist culture. The
recent trends in the People's Republic of China also point towards
this direction.

At the same time, the human component as reflected in developmental training is somewhat neglected by MNEs. Innovations in
organisation design around the "people system" do not reflect
socially relevant "modernity". The "people system" is, by and
large, still looked upon as an instrument of work, with emphasis
on the medium of material compensation, without which optimum
"work utility" cannot be obtained. The totality of the labour
force is not perceived as an organic reality where people can
feel secure with their tasks in a larger environment.

This leads us to the second observation, namely, that with a
strong accent on industrial engineering culture, the search for
alternatives for life at work and the extension of this to the
quality of life itself is almost non-existent. Employee participation is thus a non-starter in these organisations. It is
to the higher echelon of management structure only that participation in decision making and problem-solving remains confined.

This is also the watershed of work-related as well as social
exchange-related interaction among managerial cadre, supervisory
cadre and the worker cadre. Even with the best of intentions,
the technocratic culture of an innovative European automobile
producer (Volvo's Kalmar plant) failed to invoke the desirable
responses in the semi-autonomous work groups because of the omni-
potent role allocated to the computer system for the design of
which workers were passive partners. The participative culture,
at least as an expressed objective, is more accepted in the public
enterprise system than in most of the MNEs operating in India.
The implication of such development is significant for the future,
particularly because of the growing level of consciousness at the
lower echelons of a productive system with more and more induction of "new workers", even in the MNEs, as replacements for the
older generation.

Third, the business operation of the MNEs is premised on the
per capita income growth in India. Potentially India has a
large internal market to be tapped. However, the goods and
services of the MNEs are dependent on the growing but highly

skewed purchasing power reflected in effective demand.   Creation
of effective mass demand, however, has still to become a business
objective of many MNEs.   Over-all departmental strategies reflected
in improvements in the agricultural sector and the growing public
enterprise system are expected to perform that role.   Thus the
MNEs' rationale for existence is contingent upon the national plans
for growth.   Through these the market for the products of the
MNEs are to be developed so that their high value-added goods
become accepted.   The role of many MNEs in India is confined to
serve the consumer needs of the upper income strata and not the
wage-goods-needs of the largest section of the population.   It is
a matter for some reflection as to how far the MNEs can reorient
their technological base in India so as to create an infrastructure
for facilitating the growth of need-based goods and services for
the majority of people who belong to the lowest income group; and
reorient their training efforts accordingly.

Lastly, the MNEs, either at the enterprise level or at the
unit level, have the distinct advantage of being small in size
measured by the number of employees.   Despite the smallness of
size they are financially viable organisations.   Herein lies their
potential advantage.   Innovations in work structure redesign
through inculcation of participative culture are thus possible and
it is conceivable to humanise life at work to a considerable extent.
Although it might not be possible to obtain major transformation
in a qualitative sense because MNEs operate, at their best, with a
"liberalised" ideology of capitalist economic ethos, this horizon
can still be expanded.   And perhaps this may even be a way of
surviving in a changing environment.

The challenge would seem to lie in turning back to the concept of developmental training. [1] One may refer here to Bateson's
concept of the learning context.[1]   Translating the MNEs' experience into Bateson's framework, the learning ethos is characterised
by two levels which he calls "learning one and learning two".   In
the "learning one" level the context does not really change as the
technocratic ethos predominates.   People in their work-slots
acquire more and more cues to fit facts into a familiar pattern
connected to the "stimulus" of job demands and their "responses"
reflected in the price of the labour contributed.

The next higher stage, "learning two", refers to a context
which brings about a newness in consciousness and of change, and
we suggest "the why of change".   While, according to Bateson's
formulations, there are still two additional higher levels, we
find that even the "learning two" level is generally absent from
the enterprises examined in this case study.   It is thus understandable that the level at which most MNE training is undertaken
is "learning one" in which the context is regulated by job requirements as linked to wage responses.

---

[1] See Rollo May: "Gregory Bateson and Humanistic Psychology"
in Brockman, J. (ed.), <u>About Bateson</u> (New York, 1977).

A CASE STUDY ON MULTINATIONALS AND
MANPOWER TRAINING IN NIGERIA

by

Osita C. Eze[*]

Purpose and scope of the study

The purpose of this case study is to assess the contributions which multinational enterprises make to the development of local manpower in Nigeria. Since the training efforts of the multi national enterprises must in our view be examined in the light of national objectives the scope of the study will involve an evaluation of over-all government policies and legislation, as well as an examination of the role of national institutions and authorities charged with manpower development and training.

Thus, we are concerned with the nature and level of training offered by MNEs, as well as their contributions to short- and long-term development goals. In particular we shall study: the contribution of multinationals to local training efforts, how their contributions could be further strengthened where they exist, and how their contributions can be obtained where they do not exist.

Although our study of a few selected enterprises is by its nature more indicative than representative of the practice of multinationals generally, it will nevertheless assist in charting general trends.

Foreign enterprises, particularly the multinationals from the industrialised market economy countries, have in the past few decades accumulated a large reservoir of technology and knowhow.[1] Nigeria, a developing country destabilised by colonialism, possesses a totally different cultural and historical background from that found in Europe. Additionally, the wide gap that exists between Nigeria's level of development and that of advanced European countries from which Nigeria intends to obtain the various skills needed for its transformation into a modern state raises the problem of the effective transfer of skills. This is particularly reflected in the level and variety of local manpower needed for adapting the imported skills.[2]

To ensure reasonable autonomy in Nigerian manpower development various governments have introduced policies such as expatriate quota system, indigenisation measures, reform of the industrial property legislation and establishment of monitoring institutions intended to ensure greater control over and a contribution from multinationals to the general development of local manpower.

Indeed, the expatriate quota system is not only intended to ensure that jobs needing higher and middle level manpower are subsequently taken over by Nigerians, but also to provide a framework under which, through a programme of attachment or the provision of formal or informal training, Nigerians are given the opportunity to acquire the crucial qualifications needed for the creation of a skilled indigenous labour pool.

---

[*]Senior Research Fellow, Nigerian Institute of International Affairs, Lagos.

The responsibility for opinions expressed in this contribution rest solely with the author.

The policies of the various Nigerian governments in the field
of manpower development are predicated on the notion that training,
as well as other areas of development, remain primarily under the
State's direction.   These governments have adopted the philosophy
of a mixed-economy which was introduced during the colonial era.[3]
It should also be remembered that opportunities for industrialisation
available to Japan and certain former British dominions at the end
of the 19th and the beginning of the 20th century, have been closed
to Nigeria.[4]   In this context Nigeria's economic relations have
been pushed to the periphery vis-à-vis the international market
system and the basic question arises as to how multinational enterprises can contribute through transfer of skills to the over-all
economic development of Nigeria.   Accordingly, after a brief examination of the over-all Nigerian development strategy, the role will
be discussed which private enterprises including multinationals
(which represent the bulk of the industry) are expected to play in
developing local skills and Nigerian self-sufficiency.

Government policy on manpower developments

Over-all development strategy

Since independence Nigerian governments have been very much
concerned with employment creation and manpower development.   It
was not, however, until the second plan period in the 1970s that
the problem of the lopsided educational system which favoured social
sciences was directly addressed.   In this context the plan stated
that "Technical education has unfortunately not received all the
emphasis it deserves in a growing economy."[5]

This bias had certain adverse consequences.   First, it led to
the uneconomical use of the senior manpower category.   Second,
because not enough intermediate manpower was being produced there
was a growing demand by the private sector for expatriate intermediate
manpower especially in the construction, manufacturing and processing
industries.   Therefore if an economic skill-mix was to be achieved
from local sources, enrolment in technical institutes would have to
rise considerably during the plan period.   The National Manpower
Board was charged with keeping under review the enrolment ratio
between science and technology and arts and humanities both in the
universities and in technical educational institutions.

The objectives of the second plan were to: (a) contain the
incidence of youth unemployment by provision of training and employment opportunities; (b) correct educational imbalances in the
educational system consistent with the changing requirements of the
economy; (c) reduce the proportion of expatriate participation;
and (d) meet the manpower requirements and optimum development of
the economy as a whole.[6]

While there was an attempt to project manpower requirements
under the second plan it was evident that the method by which this
was sought to be achieved was highly unsatisfactory.   It is clear
that more emphasis was placed by the Nigerian Government on employment creation than on the estimation of individual categories of
manpower that needed to be trained over the plan period.[7]   It was
in fact admitted that in future manpower projection would have to
take into account, inter alia, the need for refining and further
disaggregation of employment data.   Still, the plan announced

figures reflecting additional manpower needs for the senior, intermediate, skilled and residual categories for the 1970-74 period in
selected occupations of medium and large scale industries. They
were 13,297, 32,379, 72,109 and 102,306 respectively bringing the
grand total to 220,000 additional people for all the categories
of manpower.[8]

The Third Development Plan continues the objectives of the
second plan by focusing on: (a) the expansion of employment
opportunities through the implementation of employment-oriented
programmes and the removal of constraints on the growth of employment
in various sectors of the economy; (b) introduction of industrial
attachment programmes, occupational guidance and similar schemes
which are aimed at bridging the gap between education and training
and the world of work; and (c) strengthening of existing education
and training facilities and the establishment of additional ones in
identified areas of need.   Continued emphasis is to be placed on
technical education in order to correct the imbalances of the past.
It was projected that out of the 28,843 graduates from Nigerian
universities during the period 1975-76 to 1979-80, 3,462 would come
from engineering, surveying and environmental design and 4,759 from
the natural sciences, while 1,443 would come from agricultural
science.   Economics and other social sciences would provide 3,605,
arts 2,884, education 3,577, mass communication, journalism and law
and others 1,182 graduates.   It was further predicted that the
turn out from the colleges of technology and polytechnics for the
plan period would be 29,030.[9]

Needless to say there is a direct link between the educational
infrastructure and manpower development.   Indeed the Third Plan
clearly underlines the fact that an important aspect of the labour
force is its quality.   While the quantitative aspect of manpower
development has to be taken into account, its educational and skill
content is much more important.   It must be stressed in this context
that the quality of the Nigerian labour force has improved steadily
over time as a result of the significant expansion in educational
and training activities by both government and private agencies.
The projected additional manpower needed for the senior, intermediate,
skilled, semi-skilled as well as unskilled categories in large and
medium-sized establishments for the 1975-80 plan period were 35,250,
87,300, 123,150, and 234,300 respectively, bringing the grand total
to 480,000.   This means that the projected demand is higher by
260,000 persons than the projected needs in the second plan period.

The increase in demand of various levels of manpower is not
surprising.   Apart from the expansion of economic activity resulting
primarily from Nigeria's oil wealth, and the establishment of enterprises which might not have been envisaged under the second plan
period, the projected figures for the second plan period as already
indicated, might not fully have reflected actual manpower demands.
A recent study by the Manpower Secretariat (not yet finalised) has
brought out new figures with respect to both the output of various
national educational and training institutions as well as the
additional manpower required for the periods between 1977 and 1981.

It is expected in this study that student enrolment in primary
schools will increase by a little over 3 million per annum during
the period 1978/79-80/81 and it is also expected that 1,200,000 will
finish primary school between now and 1981.   It is not clear how
many students are going to complete secondary school but there will
certainly not be enough jobs for secondary school leavers.   Student
enrolment in universities rose from 31,511 in 1975-76 to 41,400 in
1977-78, an increase of more than 25 per cent.

It might be added that the number of technical colleges increased
from 9 in 1973 to 21 in 1977-78 with a corresponding increase in
student enrolment from about 8,000 to a little over 19,000. However,
the increase in both student enrolment and turn out (in polytechnics/
colleges of technology) has been modest with respect to scientific
and technical courses including architecture, quantity surveying,
town planning, laboratory technology and engineering (civil, building,
mechanical etc.) in contrast to an increase in enrolment in management
and other non-technical courses.[10]

Despite increasing emphasis on technical education it appears
that there still might be a serious shortage of various levels of
technical and technological manpower for years to come. The
difficulties begin with the secondary schools graduates. Because
of the poor performance of students in mathematics and science and
the difficulty in obtaining the required combinations, a sufficient
number of students for admission into science based courses does
not exist. However, in an attempt to increase the output of trained
technical middle level manpower (the lack of which imposes a very
serious constraint on national developments) the Government has sent
thousands of students to training institutions in both the eastern
and western industrialised countries. Yet it is not clear to what
extent this approach has been subjected to a rigorous critical
appraisal.

The estimated additional trained manpower needed for the years
to come is expected to be supplied mainly from the various national
training and educational institutions. Additional manpower for
the various categories is also expected to come from Nigerians
trained in foreign institutions as well as by upgrading those already
working in Nigeria. Manpower forecasts for 1977-80 show that with
respect to managerial and administrative categories additional manpower requirements are expected to range between 400 (for data processing superintendents) and over 7,000 (for administrative and
executive officers, supervisors, foremen, confidential secretaries
and stenographers). For the technical, scientific and other
professional and semi-professional groups, additional manpower
requirements were highest for engineering technicians, civil and
structural engineers, electrical and electronic engineers, survey
technicians and draughtsmen (2,000 and above). The estimated
additional requirements are even higher for most of the artisan
categories (fitter mechanics etc.), i.e. over 12,000.[11] The relevance of these forecasts may, however, be affected by the uncertainty
in the tempo of economic activity resulting in part from the world
economic crisis that produces its worst effects in developing
countries particularly when the main source of revenue is one or the
other of the primary commodities, which is subject to price fluctua-
tions and often accompanied by the deterioration in terms of trade.

Training institutions

With respect to management training, special mention must be
made of the parastatal Centre for Management Development (CMD)
established under the second plan period to co-ordinate management
training and design management courses for the country. CMD does
not undertake training as such but rather acts as a management
development facilitator assisting in the training of high and intermediate level management. Other major institutions connected with
manpower training are the Industrial Training Fund (ITF) and to some
extent the National Science and Technology Development Agency (NSTDA).

The ITF was established during the second plan period to assist, inter alia, in the industrial training of indigenous personnel. The Fund was a consequence of the accelerated economic activity in the 1970s and the growing awareness of heavy reliance on foreign expertise and general manpower for the execution of Nigeria's various economic policies and projects. The Government felt, therefore, the need to institute policies which will encourage effective indigenous participation in the national economy and a reduction in the nation's dependence on foreigners.[12]

By 1972 the Fund had carried out the first phase of a training survey which showed that only a few enterprises in the country were offering any kind of training to their staff and even then training was often unplanned and unsystematic. It was found that many of the enterprises in question did not regard training as an integral part of company development policy. Furthermore the Fund found that in a large number of enterprises there was no staff specifically assigned to the training function and even where such staff existed a good number of training officers were not very knowledgeable in staff training methods.[13] Consonant with previous predictions on manpower shortages, the Fund survey also detected a critical shortage in the areas of technology and engineering, especially at the level of technicians, and crafts and semi-skilled manpower. There was also a reluctance on the part of industries to employ recent university graduates in engineering and technology on the ground that they were inexperienced.[14]

The functions of the Fund as specified in the decree establishing it are broadly formulated. Thus, the Fund does not only carry out training programmes but also co-operates with or assists others in training local personnel.

Outcome of national training efforts

While the Second Development Plan attempted to deal (albeit in a limited and imperfect manner) with employment generation and manpower objectives, shortages of the critical skills were still to be found during the Third Development Plan period. One reason advanced for this state of affairs is that although the manpower objectives of the second plan were clearly brought out, rather few specific programmes to achieve these goals were established by the plan. Furthermore, the employment implications of individual projects were generally not identified. Additionally there was usually no clear quantification of functional relationships, between training, employment, and development apart from the general assumption that the growth in national income, favoured by high inputs in capital projects would result in an expected growth in employment.[15]

Shortage in the various categories of manpower, particularly technical occupations continues to impose constraints on the implementation of national policies and objectives. The vacancy rate of 1 April 1977 for civil and structural engineers and for chemical engineering technicians and mining engineering technicians was estimated to be over 50 per cent. In addition there seems to be insufficient numbers of candidates for admission to science based courses in universities, colleges of technology/polytechnics and other specialised institutions including advanced and technical teacher colleges, etc.[16]

What seems to be lacking in the country's planning efforts is a technology plan that could form an integral part of the national development plan. Both the Nigerian Council for Science and Technology (established in 1970) and its successor organisation, the National Science and Technology Development Agency,[17] (NSTDA) did not produce such a plan although one of the Council's functions is "to determine priorities for scientific activities in the federation in relation to the economic and social policies of the country".[18]

Thus in the Third Development Plan, although technical training was emphasised, no analysis was made regarding the technology needed to implement it. The Council did, however, prepare in 1975 a document entitled National Policies and Priorities for Research and Technology[19] which dealt in a fragmented way with science and technology and related manpower training. In view of these difficulties, in part attributable to structural problems, the Council[20] was replaced by the NSTDA.

The NSTDA came into being in 1977 and has not yet formulated a master plan on science and technology. The process of formulating such a plan has, however, been set in motion. It can be expected that such a plan will analyse technological matters such as the technological implications of investments, the mode of transfer of technology, and the role of consultancy services and subcontracting in developing local skills.

Finally mention may be made of the newly created National Office of Industrial Property established within the Ministry of Industry, intended to be responsible for evaluating the technological contents of investments. The unpackaging process that this would involve will afford further training for local personnel. The Office is still being organised and has not as of yet taken off.

Role of multinational enterprises
within the framework of government
policy

The first Nigerian development plan did not articulate the role which the private sector, including the multinationals, was to play in the development of local manpower. With the liberal attitude towards private foreign investments and enterprises it was felt that the encouragement of the transfer of capital from abroad would also bring with it as a by-product, the training of local manpower. However, it was realised eventually that if multinationals are to aid in the achievement of national development goals there was a need for greater direction and control of their activities.

Initially, this goal was approached by marginal reforms to the industrial property system, based essentially on the principles of the Paris Convention more concerned with the protection of private property than with the safeguarding of national interests. This policy was followed by two indigenisation decrees, the first in 1972 and the second in 1977.[21] The first decree affected only certain categories of enterprises, while the second decree related to all enterprises in which Nigerians owned varying percentages of shares and held some positions at the managerial and directorial levels.

It was indeed realised that with indigenisation it was imperative to have a pool of local manpower to participate not only in the management but also in the ownership of the new enterprises. The ITF, created about the time of the first indigenisation efforts, was

to have a prominent place in these policies,[22] in particular regarding the training of local manpower required for indigenisation
efforts.   Thus the Fund currently imposes an annual levy of 1 per
cent of the total payroll of enterprises employing 25 and more
workers.   Where the Fund is satisfied with training, development and consultancy services in industry, 60 per cent of the
contributions can be retained for the financing of these activities.
The Fund also makes ex gratia payments that range from 1 per cent
to 10 per cent to contributors that have effective in-plant training
facilities.   Both local and foreign enterprises are subjected to
these policies.   In connection with the Nigerian Enterprises
Promotion Decree of 1977, the Honourable Commissioner J. Garba stated
that the indigenisation policy was designed "to blend indigenous
enterprise and capital with foreign technology and know-how."[23]
The policy of ushering in joint ventures between local entrepreneurs
and multinational enterprises is essentially geared to facilitate
such an acquisition of both technological and managerial skills.

Training in selected multinational enterprises

In this section the types and volume of various training programmes, their relevance for their employees and the economy as a
whole in four sample enterprises will be reviewed.   These were
surveyed through interviews with various knowledgeable persons,
in particular management of the enterprises; workers and trade
union leaders and competent government officials.   The interviews
in question were both formal and informal.   Additionally, engineering consultants and managers of the local private sector were also
contacted for complementary and comparative information.   In the
following analysis the views of the various groups will be systematically recounted only where this provides particular insight into
an issue area.

The multinational enterprises in the survey have the following
characteristics:

Enterprise A is a joint venture between Nigerian interests with
40 per cent shareholding, and a construction firm based in the F.R. of
Germany, with the remaining 60 per cent of the shares. Negotiations
are apparently going on to increase Nigerian shareholdings in the
joint venture. The enterprise is one of the largest construction companies operating in Nigeria.   As of 31 March 1979 the company's
employees numbered 11,052 of which 312 held senior technical and
administrative positions.   Of this latter category, 193 or almost
two-thirds, are expatriates.[24]   The company has no formal agreement
with the Nigerian Government for training manpower although it
co-operates with the Industrial Training Fund (ITF) by providing for
attachment of engineers in their construction work, especially
during the vacation period.   It also provides training for a few
Nigerian engineers overseas and on-the-job training for Nigerian
engineers and technicians.   Research and development facilities are
limited to testing, virtually all of which is carried out in a laboratory in Nigeria, where a Nigerian is in charge.

The Chairman of the joint venture company is a Nigerian as are
three of the six managing directors.[25]   At the professional level
there were originally thirteen engineers, five of whom resigned and
have not been replaced.   Out of the remaining eight, four are
Nigerians.   At the engineering technical level there are about
23 Nigerians and 7 expatriates.   These are normally site engineers
and site managers.   The senior supervisory posts (supervisors and
senior foremen) are all occupied by Nigerians.

While one may notice a substantial degree of Nigerianisation
and training, there are certain shortcomings regarding the enterprises' contribution to local manpower development.   First, there
is no organised formal training for any category of local manpower.
Second, despite the fact that the company provides some on-the-job
training for various categories of workers, there still seems to be
a great potential for the training of Nigerians in higher level
technology.   It must be added that it has been company practice to
import most of its inputs, including prefabricated concrete blocks
or slabs from abroad.   The reason given for the virtual absence of
organised high and intermediate level training is the cyclical
nature of the work done by construction firms as opposed to enterprises engaged in manufacturing.   Thus, in spite of the Government's
policy of attaching engineers from the Ministry of Works to construction firms, Nigerians have not been trained in sufficient numbers
for the proper maintenance of the roads constructed by the enterprise
in question.

The enterprise seems to be somewhat an exception in this connection as it is known that other enterprises dealing with the
maintenance of heavy construction equipment, have trained Nigerian
mechanics which after several years did most of the required work
although under the supervision of expatriates.   Several of the
interviewed workers of enterprise A indicated that they had benefited
from the "learning by doing" obtained from the enterprise.   But
most of them did not consider their career prospects satisfactory
since this training did not allow them to rise beyond the level of
foreman.   In the opinion of government officers interviewed,
enterprise A could make a more meaningful contribution to the development of Nigerian manpower in the construction industry and this
should be possible especially in co-operation with the local
institutions.

Enterprise B is a subsidiary of an important car producer in
the Federal Republic of Germany and employs about 3,000 persons
(there is some Nigerian participation).   The enterprise has a
training centre which started operation in 1974 one year before the
factory commenced production.   The entrants are school certificate
holders and are trained for three years in various crafts.   The
centre trains electricians, automobile engineers, fitters, machinists,
plumbers and also various categories of salesmen.   The trainees sit
for government trade tests (levels two and three) conducted by the
Ministry of Labour and two groups of trainees comprised of 25 each
have since completed their training.   There is no doubt that these
categories of manpower are critical for the operation of the factory
as well as for the Nigerian economy as a whole.   The enterprise
seems to have an open policy regarding the professional choice of
the trainees, i.e. it does not insist that they stay with the
enterprise.   For this reason an expansion of the programmes in
question would be beneficial for the country.   Trainees interviewed,
indicated that the programme had improved over time especially since
theoretical training had been combined with on-the-job training and
additional instructors had been hired.

The situation seems to be somewhat different at the supervisory
level. Here Nigerians are not given systematic training and the
same seems to be the case for higher-level engineers. Thus, these
positions are mostly held by expatriates. Management holds that it
takes too long to train local higher-level engineers whose work
would include final assembly, production planning, and construction
and service engineering. It is noted, however, that these local
skills are critical if the cars are to be truly "made in Nigeria".

While there is no specific agreement with the company for the transfer of technology and management skills to Nigerians, there is the general understanding that the enterprise will train Nigerians in order that they may take over practically all operations in the future although there seems to be no detailed time schedule for this. Likewise it is intended that production inputs should be progressively made in Nigeria. Managements believe that there are advantages in using local materials, where available. Roofing materials, paints, grease, seat materials, some chemicals and tyres produced in Nigeria are already being used. On the other hand, attempts to use locally manufactured batteries failed because they did not meet the required standards. Local inputs are purchased from enterprises registered in Nigeria. It is envisaged to systematically subcontract the production of car parts to such companies.

The management of enterprise B estimates that it should be possible to produce in Nigeria the entire car body and engines in twenty years time. This seems to depend, however, on the functioning of the Ajokuta steel complex. In addition the facilities for pressing and fabricating car engines locally still have to be created. There is no research and development in enterprise B except for a laboratory for quality control manned by Nigerians under the supervision of expatriates.

Higher management and technical positions of the enterprise are overwhelmingly in the hands of expatriates. While the chairman is a Nigerian, the Germans provide the managing director and technical expertise. They also own a majority of the shares. There are four divisions: production, marketing, finance and administration and supplies, all headed by Germans without Nigerian counterparts. Out of the nineteen departmental heads only five are Nigerians. The bulk of the Nigerian employees are semi-skilled or unskilled labourers. One main reason for this may be that the car industry is very young in Nigeria.

Enterprise C is a subsidiary of a UK enterprise in the food and beverages sector employing about 3,000 people. There is considerable Nigerian shareholding. The enterprise is reputed to have one of the best training programmes in the country with a special training centre in the factory. Training provided covers the full range from that for factory hands and middle level workers, to that for higher level manpower. On-the-job training is provided for manual skills such as plumbers, electricians and mechanics. About 80 technicians are trained every year both for the Lagos and Benin breweries of the enterprise. Training is also provided within the company for secretarial and clerical staff. The enterprise opened a new training centre in Benin in 1978 and intends to build an entirely new modern training facility in Lagos in view of the expanding Nigerian brewing industry.[26] Most of those trained tend to remain with the company although there is no formal requirement that they should serve the company after being trained.

Training provided by enterprise C for high management cadres comprises two courses: a management appreciation course and a management development course. The courses include leadership and motivation appraisal system, communication and industrial relations.[27] Some of the Nigerians are sent overseas to be trained in brewery schools in the United Kingdom, United States and West Germany. All the brewing managers, who normally have B.Sc. degrees, are Nigerians. It would therefore appear that production could be run completely by Nigerians. The chairman is a Nigerian, the general manager is an expatriate and out of the seven managers of the enterprise four are Nigerians.

The enterprise undertakes some major research and development in Nigeria geared to improving brewing techniques. The processing lines have been reorganised by Nigerian engineers. In addition, research is being conducted into the possible use of local raw materials in the brewing of beer. For the moment mostly Nigerian water is used. The enterprise has received a refund from the ITF since it was satisfied with the existing training programme.

Enterprise D is a construction company established as a joint venture between an Italian firm and the Nigerian Government. The agreement between the Federal Government of Nigeria and the Italian enterprise contains specific, although rather general, provisions on training, which provide that "at the end of the first year of the registration of the company (i.e. the Italian partner) shall establish a training programme directed towards enabling the company to accelerate the employment of Nigerian personnel in engineering, management and supervisory grades". Indeed five officers arrived from Italy in 1970 to train Nigerians as artisans, technical and administrative managers and as engineers (mechanical engineers, quantity surveyors, material and soil engineers, site engineers and project engineers). Other main occupational categories are accountants, cost accountants, chief buyers and artisans. In 1978 21 Nigerians were trained in these occupations. The course curricula are rather detailed and are apparently intended to combine theoretical training with practical experience.[28]

While the training efforts of the enterprise are rather impressive, their contribution to local manpower development is hampered by failure (of the enterprise) to designate specific jobs for the trainees as well as to specify the senior persons to whom they are attached. It should also be noted that the laboratory programme does not usually involve Nigerian engineers. The Nigerian trainees have in fact petitioned the management about the inadequacy of the situation. In this enterprise which is 60 per cent owned by Nigerians and in which the Nigerian Government nominates 6 out of the 10 directors (although the managing director is appointed by the Italian partner) it might be expected that Nigerian training interests would be more vigorously pursued. But as in many enterprises in which Nigerians hold considerable shares, those who represent Nigerian interests apparently often need to show more concern for the development of local manpower required for the country.

Contribution of MNEs to local training efforts

The basic policy of the Nigerian Government, as already indicated, is that wherever qualified Nigerians are available they should be employed. In the absence of qualified personnel local manpower should be trained to gradually replace expatriates. The establishment of the system of expatriate quota was precisely motivated by the need to encourage the training of local manpower at various levels for the purposes of replacing expatriate workers. Indeed the degree to which trained Nigerians can replace expatriates in the jobs requiring critical skills for the country is a measure of the success or failure of the training programmes. It is also

indicative, therefore, of the extent to which multinationals can
contribute to the development of Nigerian self-reliance in the field
of manpower.

However, it was found in our analysis that, globally-speaking,
there was no significant change by the end of the second plan period
in the level of expatriate employment.   The reasons for this were,
the absence of a precise machinery for allocating expatriate quotas,
a liberal policy towards firms involved in construction projects
and the ability of firms to continue in various ways to renew the
quota indefinitely.[29]   Yet the application of the expatriate quota
is based on a set of conditions: (a) first, where a business has
not already been established, the enterprise has to apply for a
business permit; (b) second, a separate application is to be made
for the employment of a number of expatriates with specified skill/
qualification/job experience; (c) third, an application has to be
made by an individual expatriate to take up a position in an enterprise approved as above; (d) finally, the individual expatriate
also has to apply for entry visa and residence permit when he accepts
a job granted under (c) above.   While the first application relates
to matters of finance and industrial policy, the second and third
are based on manpower considerations.   The immigration laws obviously
provide a final check on the admission of expatriate personnel who
intend to work in Nigeria.[30]   Since various ministries are involved,
and in order to avoid delays in processing applications for expatriate quota, it was thought that a business advisory committee
composed of representatives from the relevant ministries should advise
the Commissioner for Internal Affairs which is ultimately responsible
for the administration of the system.   This does not seem to have
materialised fully as various ministries still deal with their own
particular aspects of the problem.

It was found that during the second plan period the objectives
of phasing out the expatriate quota in the shortest possible time
in the building and construction industry failed because no system
had evolved to accomplish this objective.   Efforts were to be made
in the third plan to tie all existing and future expatriate quota
allocations strictly to the training of Nigerian counterparts.   It
was, however, evident in the absence of schedules for the indigenisation of personnel and effective supervisory machinery in this
context that little would be achieved.   It would appear also that
the high growth rate, especially in the construction and building
industries in past years did not lead to a correlary expansion of
the training of Nigerians in the supervisory and professional grades
through on-the-job training.   Thus there is a deficit of Nigerians
who, on a continuous basis, can train various categories of manpower.

A Nigerianisation enterprise agency was to be established early
in the third plan under the auspices of the National Manpower Board
in consultation with the relevant agencies of the Government.   All
enterprises would have been required to submit to this agency their
programmes for phasing-out expatriates.   The detailed provisions
conceived in this respect for the regulation of the expatriate workforce never materialised.[31]

Although the ITF does in fact supervise students on attachment
and sends out questionnaires to ascertain the nature and level of
training programmes in various industries, it can only use the power
of persuasion and inducement to encourage the institution to provide
training programmes.

Without further influence by the Government it would appear from the present case study that multinational enterprises tend to train and transfer mainly the basic skills needed for their own operations. Specific national policies seem required to ensure that they contribute in a more meaningful way to the process of skill development for national planning policies. Apart from enterprise C, which as we have seen has a comprehensive training and research and development programme, the other three enterprises surveyed fall, in varying degrees, short of the objectives that national priorities would require. None of the three enterprises is, for instance, engaged in the training of high level manpower needed for research and development. But the Government has to give more guidance in this process. There is, as already mentioned, an urgent need for the formulation of a national technology plan as an integral part of the over-all plan that would provide the framework for the operations of the multinationals. In addition, the expatriate quota would need to be more rigorously enforced and geared towards the training of Nigerians to replace expatriates. There should be power vested in the relevant state authority to enforce compliance or impose penalties for non-compliance.

Another policy option would be the inclusion of specific training provisions in all agreements between the Nigerian Government and foreign MNEs. Presently there exist formal agreements for training between the Nigerian Government on the one hand and enterprise A, B and D on the other, but they are not explicit enough. Furthermore, the directors representing Nigerian interests on the board of directors of the foreign enterprises (joint ventures) should be carefully selected so they can wield real influence.

So as to develop further the critical technical skills and the country's innovative capacity, it would seem important that MNEs promote their research and development function in Nigeria as well as their links with local industry and research and development institutions. Representatives of the various enterprises interviewed seemed ready to improve and expand their training programmes; but to do this in a meaningful way for the country, the indicated guidance from and co-operation with the Nigerian authorities seems required. It must also be noted in this context that available information on the training and utilisation of Nigerian manpower is not complete.[32] Some of the existing evidence seems to suggest both underemployment and malemployment of critical skills. Nigeria might in the end find out that she has more productive manpower than she really believes.

Summary

Both the Nigerian Government and the MNEs surveyed undertake appreciable training efforts. But this does not seem to be enough for the future. The Government, aware that multinationals are in general reluctant to transfer skills needed for full autonomy of subsidiary operations, has adopted over time certain measures and policies to improve the situation. These measures need to be further developed through comprehensive planning, including a technology plan, and institutions that can effectively supervise and enforce government policies in the field of manpower development.[33] This will help to minimise the present gap between declared national objectives and concrete achievements in the pursuance of greater self-reliance as a goal for economic and manpower policies.

Notes

[1] Osita C. Eze: "Multinationals and manpower in Tanzania", in Journal of World Trade Law, Sept.-Oct. 1977, pp. 446 ff.

[2] See Osita C. Eze: "Programme of action for strengthening technological capacity in Africa", in Transfer of Technology and African Development. (Turku Peace Research Group, forthcoming.)

[3] B. Onimode and E. Osagie: Economic Interpretation of Nigeria's Draft Constitution, unpublished paper, p. 18.

[4] Archie Mafeje: Science, Ideology and Development (Uppsala, Scandinanvian Institute of African Studies, 1978), p. 15.

[5] Second National Development Plan 1970-74 (Lagos, Federal Ministry of Information, 1970), p. 316.

[6] ibid., p.311.

[7] ibid., pp.329-330. For an analysis of the problems of manpower forecasting in Nigeria see H.N. Pandit: Forecasting Manpower Needs for Economic Development of Nigeria, paper presented at the National Conference on Manpower Constraints to Nigeria's Development, University of Lagos, 19-22 Dec. 1978.

[8] Second Development Plan, op. cit.

[9] Third National Development Plan 1975-80, Vol. 1 (Lagos, Federal Ministry of Economic Development), pp. 376 and 387.

[10] National Manpower Secretariat: Current Manpower Demand and Supply Situation, background paper for National Conference on Manpower Constraints to Nigeria's Economic Development, University of Lagos, 19-22 Dec. 1978, pp. 73-79. See also I.O. Oladapo: Manpower Requirements for Engineering and Technology and Allied Disciplines, paper presented at the National Conference on Manpower Constraints to Nigeria's Economic Development, 28 Jan.-1 Feb. 1979.

[11] Current Manpower Demand, op. cit., table 13.

[12] Industrial Training Fund in Perspective (Nigeria, Barka Press Limited), pp. 3 ff. See also Industrial Training Fund Decree No. 42 of 1971.

[13] Industrial Training Fund in Perspective op. cit., pp. 5-6.

[14] ibid., p. 7. See also A.B. Fafunwa: "Education both as enabling and disenabling factor in development", paper presented at the National Conference on Manpower Constraints to Nigeria's Economic Development, University of Lagos, 29 Jan.-1 Feb. 1979.

15 Guidelines for the Third National Development Plan 1975-1980 (Lagos, Federal Ministry of Economic Development and Reconstruction), p. 49.

16 See ibid. and Current Manpower Demand and Supply Situation, op. cit., pp. 23, 80.

17 Nigerian Council for Science and Technology Decree, No. 6 of 1970; National Science and Technology Development Agency Decree, No. 5 of 1977.

18 Decree No. 6 of 1970, sections 2 and 3.

19 Council Report (Lagos, NCST Secretariat, Cabinet Office, 1975).

20 There was an imbalance in the composition of the council leading to scientists being by far outnumbered. The chairman had no political status or leverage and the secretary was a bureaucrat.

21 Nigerian Enterprises Promotion Decree, No. 4 of 1972. Nigerian Enterprises Promotion Decree, No. 3 of 1977.

22 Industrial Training Fund in Perspective, op. cit., p. 5.

23 Cited in Osita C. Eze: Multinationals and Nigeria, an unpublished paper.

24 See Sunday Times (Nigeria), 5 Aug. 1979, p. 6.

25 ibid. There were two Nigerian managing directors out of five.

26 Annual Report and Accounts of Enterprise C, 1978.

27 A comprehensive syllabus for the training of various categories of local manpower is currently being worked out.

28 See the course curricula in the appendix of this case study.

29 Guidelines for the Third National Development Plan, 1975-80, op. cit., p. 54.

30 ibid.

31 ibid., p. 55.

32 Necessary breakdowns by category of trainees are frequently missing; see Current Manpower Demand, op. cit., pp. 85-86.

33 See Osita C. Eze: An International Code of Conduct on the Transfer of Technology; A Third World Perspective. Paper presented at a seminar at the Nigerian Institute of International Affairs, Lagos, 7 June 1979.

Appendix to the Nigerian case study

Course curricula of Enterprise D
a joint venture in the construction industry

Teaching programme for
technical managers

Primary site school

For technicians all together (site engineer, deputy agent,
soil mechanic engineer).

The main purpose of this primary school of the course, for the
first phase of the training programme concerned (the foreseen
duration of which is two months), is to recall to the trainee's
mind the general principles of design and road construction, to
appraise the individual's ability in order to suitably direct him
for the secondary site school and in the meantime to become familiar
with the trainee's mentality, his degree of preparation, psychology
and sense of duty.

The primary site school's development shall be mainly theoretical with lectures during the morning and relevant investigations
on the spot during the afternoon.

At the end an opinion will be given and a selection will be
made to place the trainees in the appropriate stream for the
secondary site school.

Teaching programme

- Principles of company's organisation.

- Preliminary design of the roads: general principles; road
  classification; method for economical selection of the road's
  layouts and profiles; geometrical and geological references.
  The road: profiles and cross-sections; embankment, sub-base,
  base course, binder and wearing course; bridges and culverts.
  Soil mechanics: soil classification, empirical identification
  of the various materials; general criteria for the investigation of borrow-pits for embankment, sub-base and base course.
  Grading. Laboratory tests for the identification of the
  soils. General knowledge of the asphaltic concrete.

- Cement concrete - general knowledge; classes and mixing of
  concrete. Tests on concrete: slump test, cubes, etc;
  description.

- Production planning.

Secondary site school

Divided into two groups viz: first group - for site engineer,
agent and deputy agent, project engineer; second group - for soil
mechanics engineer and geologists.

This site school will last ten months. The trainees will

rotate between in-depth study of problems in theoretical lectures
(to be held in the afternoon) and practical training on the spot
during the morning. During the course the trainees will write
essays about their site experience.

At the end of the school, the trainees will take an examination.
The final grading will qualify trainees to proceed with training
abroad for the second phase.

Teaching programme

First group - For site engineer, agent and deputy agent, project
              engineer.

- Final design for roads: plans and profiles, cross-sections
  altimetry, curves and easing of curves, distances for transportation of materials.

- Structures: bridges, box and pipe culverts: design. Concrete,
  direct foundations and piles foundations.

- Preliminary programme. Gant's diagram.

- Machinery and equipment. Types and their use, cycles,
  production team, job's economy. Scrapers, graders, bulldozers,
  excavators, compactors, pay loaders, trucks, paving machines.
  Lifting equipment and for piling.

- Plant: crushing plant, mixing plant, batching plant and asphalt
  plant.

- Organisation of the site and forecast of the jobs. Personnel's
  schedule.

- Final programme: the Pert.

- Technical and administrative studies in connection with the job's
  carrying out: qualitative and quantitative selection of the
  equipment, depreciation, consumption, spares, hourly costs.
  Forecast of labour.

- Tendering: specifications and conditions of contract. Prime
  costs and own cost, financing, general expenses - budgeting,
  contingencies and profit, pricing and bill of quantities.

- Fulfilment of the job: technical and economical criteria for
  material's selection, sources and timing of supplying, principles
  of supplying, stock supply.

- Human relations and administration of the personnel.

- Job management: adjustment of the programmes by time, quantity
  surveying, costing.

- Contract management: general conditions of contract, relationship with the employer, claims, technical and administrative
  formalities.

- Budget, inventory, evaluation of the stocks, end of the contract.

Second group - For soil mechanic engineers.

- The soil laboratory's sections: earth, stone, concrete, bitumen and asphalt.

- Soils: laboratory's equipment and tests.   Soil classification: sieve analysis, specific gravity, optimum moisture content. Proctor test (standard and modified). Atteberg limits: liquid limit, plastic limit, plasticity index.   The graphical representation of the laboratory test, envelopes, diagrams.

- The materials for embankment, for sub-base, for base-courses.

- The job checking and on-site tests.   Sampling and relations between the laboratory results and the real job execution.

- The asphalt concrete for road paving.   Stability and flow: bitumen content and index of void.   Marshall test.

- Setting of asphalt plants: drawing of the samples along the road and relation with the laboratory results.

- The concretes.   Classes of concrete, strengths, trial mix, batching, additives, vibration, workability, slump tests. Cubes: manufacturing, curing (times and methods), compression test.

- The laboratory management, relationship between the laboratory, the site and the employer.

CHAPTER V

CONCLUSIONS

The evidence compiled for this study suggests that multi-national enterprises (MNEs) undertake a considerable amount of training in developing countries. Most of this training, as well as training at headquarters, is conducted to satisfy staffing requirements essential for the functioning of the enterprise and is of a rather specialised nature. Such training does, therefore, not always explicitly take into account the wider and more diverse national manpower priorities of the various developing countries in which MNEs are established. Still, since many of the activities of MNEs in developing countries are in sectors important for industrial modernisation and technological growth, much of their present formal and informal training efforts certainly make a contribution to development although the term development needs to be scrutinized more closely in this connection. Often the concepts of the contribution by MNEs to economic growth and of their contribution to local training goals are not very clearly distinguished. Obviously, the latter one is the more appropriate benchmark for judging the local relevance of the training efforts of MNEs; and the application of these terms leads to some important qualification of the preceding broad assessment.

Although the volume and quality of training by MNEs is important and extends to all categories of their personnel, the training efforts are uneven and emphasize the categories thought to be of particular interest to the operations of the enterprises in a foreign environment. The training given depends a good deal on production techniques, sector, length of involvement in a country, the qualifications of the available indigenous manpower and local training policies, to which other factors, such as the business culture and role perception of the enterprises could be added. Despite these factors, which vary from situation to situation, a major emphasis in practically all of the enterprises surveyed (in terms of training resources used) is on training programmes for higher- and medium-level managerial staff and for technical "cadres" considered to be the key personnel for the optimal functioning of the enterprise. The training for manual workers (especially un- and semi-skilled) is usually less developed although in terms of numbers it represents the bulk of MNE training efforts.

Most of this training for these production workers seems to be geared towards complementing existing skills as required for the immediate performance of a specific production-line function in the enterprise ensuring a short-run return on the training investment. Such training is often brief and mainly on the job. It is usually more specific than in local enterprises and sometimes of limited use in the wider national labour market (low occupational mobility) and for the career development of the workers within the enterprise. In line with its specific task-related nature, manual worker training is conducted, as a rule by the local subsidiary in the developing host country.

The training of skilled workers, which is normally provided only for a small portion of the labour force, appears to be generally of high calibre and also of considerable value in the national labour market. This category of workers tends to absorb the largest proportion of funds made available by MNEs for training locally. Apprenticeship training is likewise reported to be of an appreciative volume in the majority of the enterprises, meeting recognised standards and often going beyond the immediate needs of the MNE.

Although MNEs utilise local management institutes or offer regional training courses in developing countries for general managers and administrative staff, most of the senior management training seems to be conducted at headquarters. The same is true for attachment programmes, together with high-level technological training, which take place either in the parent enterprise or in subsidiaries of the group in other industrialised countries.

Although the training programmes of MNEs are complementary to the locally dispensed training and thus influenced, as mentioned before, by the availability of the various categories of locally trained personnel (the quantity and quality of which generally seems to be increasing over time in most of the developing countries where MNEs are established) this apparently has not led a slowdown of MNE training efforts. Still, the availability of well-trained workers, and by implication of appropriate local training institutions (e.g., for general education, management development or vocational training), is for instance in some circumstances an important element of MNE's investment decisions in the so-called "newly industrialising countries" for labour- and skill-incentive production processes. Such international "manpower sourcing" of MNEs can be an incentive for countries to further develop their training systems. In some cases it seems to have led to competition between national and international enterprises for trained manpower and, occasionally, to imbalances in the labour market.

Depending on the level of development of a particular country, the formal training provided by the MNE, often in co-operation with local bodies frequently includes, for people from rural areas, the acquisition of basic educational skills (reading, writing, arithmetic, hygiene, etc.). This type of training is offered especially during the intial stages of establishing subsidiaries (independent of the product being manufactured). Although it appears to be diminishing in proportion over time, segments of the population previously outside the industrial sector will continue to need basic training for their socialisation and transition to an industrial society (e.g. assistance with settlement, housing and relations with authorities).

One of the reported areas of concern for MNE has been the fear of excessive staff turnover to other enterprises or government and the consequential loss of considerable training investments. Former trainees also often set up their own business, certainly a positive factor for the countries' development. The combination of training and career planning, an area not fully discussed in the sources used, could reduce this phenomenon. It has also been noted that an obligation to keep trainees on the payroll may be a discentive for MNEs to extend their training programmes. It has been mentioned, however, that while MNEs may lose trained personnel, they also gain personnel trained by other enterprises and by public training institutions. MNEs will find that both in their own long-term self-interest as well as in the development interests of their country of implantation each multinational cannot create its own

independent labour market. As training efforts at all levels grow
to the extent that various national and enterprise training efforts
can be made complementary, the chances increase for the development
of a functioning national labour market for all skill categories
without too many "technological enclaves and sectoral imbalances".

The level of skills present in a country is also an important
conditioning factor for the indigenisation programmes of governments.
Legislation, especially expatriate quota systems and the training
tax appear to have been effective in this respect. Influenced by
these, MNE training programmes have often been specifically designed
to facilitate the localisation of personnel; and the progress made
in the past decade or so with the replacement of expatriates, in the
MNEs for which relevant data are available, has been on the whole
quite impressive. On the other hand, the enterprises are still
criticised in some developing countries for not making quicker
progress with the localisation of personnel, especially with regard
to higher technical and management positions. From the enterprises'
point of view factors such as skills, the advantages of managers
from different cultures, the broader range of experience, questions
of company loyalty and, in particular, technological innovation,
are variables influencing their perceived needs for the continued
use of a certain number of expatriates thought at times difficult
to reduce further. These increasingly include, however, according
to enterprise reports, persons from other developing countries, to
be considered under the aspect of "brain-drain" from these
countries. It could not be exactly determined from the available
data which proportion such persons hold in the expatriate category.
It seems, nevertheless, that the international managerial elites of
the MNEs are still mainly composed of home country staff and also
staff from other industrialised countries.

Several enterprises underline in this context the aspect of
innovation. In their view the accelerated introduction of new
production technologies and management techniques require sometimes
even a (temporary) increase in the number of expatriate staff;
in part also for instructing local staff. Finally, it must be
recalled that the use of expatriates in enterprises is not
particular to multinationals - expatriates are also employed by
domestic enterprises of developing host countries. This shows that
the localisation problems have a more general dimension.

It is not surprising, in this context, that developing countries
often wish that MNEs would contribute more resources to the training
of local middle and upper level managers over and above the
immediate needs of the companies, in the hope that MNEs will share
their international management experience more with the local
enterprises. Although considerable possibilities still seem to be
given for this purpose, a number of limiting factors must also be
recognised, such as the enterprise-specific nature of training by
MNEs, and the expensive character of some of it when it is conducted
at regional and headquarters levels. Still, greater association of
MNEs with the relevant training efforts of national training
institutions yield promising results, as existing arrangements of
this type suggest.

As mentioned in several of the sources, a certain predisposi-
tion of MNEs to model, at least initially, their training activities
in developing countries after concepts employed in the home country
of the parent (perhaps seen as best fitting the enterprise worldwide)
may be potentially dysfunctional for the relevance of the training

in the developing host country. The ability, perceived need and
willingness to adapt training to local situations varies. Clearly,
appropriate adaptation is in the interest of local development but
also a consideration for the long-term viability of the enterprises
themselves in the foreign context. This has led in some enterprises to headquarter's training simulations of the particular
conditions in certain developing countries.

A connected point is the unfamiliarity of some MNEs with the
local training system and labour markets in the occasional non-
recognition, or downgrading, of local diplomas or their equivalent.
In addition, some MNEs do not seem to issue proficiency certificates
or these may only be recognised by other subsidiaries of the group
since the nature of the training was too enterprise-oriented.
Also relevant for the question of MNEs development contribution is,
obviously, the entire complex of in-plant training (favoured by
MNEs) versus training by central institutions which, as a rule,
deliver more generally recognised training and certificates.

The considerations offered in these conclusions point to the
need for intensified training co-operation between local training
institutions of the developing host countries and MNEs in
conjunction, where appropriate, with employers' and workers'
organisations, as critical factors to increase mutual benefits.[1]
Better knowledge of local training facilities can be a help for
MNEs to modify their own specific training programmes; conversely
the local institutions can find out in greater detail about the
specific contributions that can be expected from the MNEs. It is
known from the materials examined that such co-operation already
exists in various forms; but it is also known that many enterprises have not yet fully developed their relations with local
institutions.

The question of co-operation with MNEs in developing countries
seems presently to be left very much to individual initiatives
taken by local subsidiaries of MNEs on the one hand and local
training institutions on the other. Since this matter is, thus,
usually not the object of general policies at the government or
enterprise level, there is much variation in the type and scope of
such co-operation. Greater involvement of MNE headquarters and of
national-level authorities in this would be desirable. As greater
co-operation in training is a world-wide challenge, MNEs should
assess their over-all training activities at all levels in
developing countries. The total training effort in a developing
country should be of particular concern to the company as a whole, not
only for the purpose of training to meet immediate company needs
(which are determined at subsidiary level), but also for
establishing factors by which the positive effects of MNE activities
will be increasingly judged. Naturally, discretion of subsidiary
management regarding modalities should be maintained and full
consideration given to its evaluation.

Most governments treat MNEs and national enterprises alike in
training, even though, on the other hand, they may have detailed
investment regulations for foreign enterprises. While such non-
discrimination is appreciated by MNEs, it appears that the specific

---

[1] This is an area highlighted in the Tripartite Declaration of
Principles concerning Multinational Enterprises and Social Policy,
adopted by the Governing Body of the International Labour Office,
16 November 1977 (Geneva, ILO, 1977), especially paras. 29-32.

contribution which MNEs can make both to formal and informal training in the host country because of their world-wide experience and resources, is frequently neglected in the process; and the place which MNEs can hold in the national training efforts is often not sufficiently and specifically defined.

On the other hand, in some of the case studies especially, there is a tendency to request from MNEs a training contribution which seems to be over-dimensional in comparison to their main purpose, i.e. economic activity, and sometimes tends to put the MNEs on a similar footing with national training institutions (and public enterprises) which by definition have broader training functions. It is clear that prime responsibility for training in the national context must remain with government; and that the relationship between governmental efforts and those of MNEs must be seen as complementary, corresponding sometimes to parallel and sometimes to different requirements, all of which need to be co-ordinated. It is the role of governments to give guidance for the place of MNEs will have to assume in the local training efforts, in particular in national development plans and policies. The complementary role of MNEs needs to be defined in relation to all relevant actors in the local environment, which include national training institutions, public enterprises as well as large and small private enterprises, both national and multinational.

ANNEX I

<u>RESEARCH PROJECT: TRAINING PRACTICES OF</u>
<u>MULTINATIONAL ENTERPRISES AND THEIR IMPACT ON DEVELOPMENT</u>

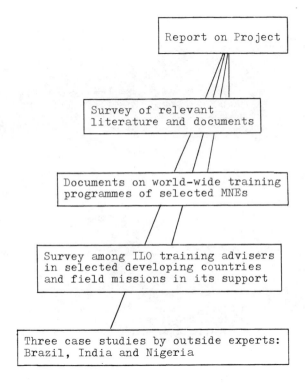

ANNEX II

Guide for ILO chief technical advisers

A.   Objectives of the research project

     The research project is part of the work programme 1978/79 of
the ILO unit responsible for multinational enterprises (MULTI).
It is undertaken in collaboration with the ILO's Training Department (FORM), external collaborators and the International Institute
for Labour Studies (INST).

     The project aims at an evaluation of the degree to which train-
ing furnished by MNEs corresponds not only to the immediate needs
for these enterprises but contributes equally to the general training needs of developing countries.

     More precisely, there is a need to evaluate the extent to
which the training furnished by MNEs develops useful skills and
favours career possibilities, helps to resolve bottlenecks in
national training efforts and, in a more general way, is in harmony
with the objectives, programmes and priorities of national development.

     The project will use three main sources of information:

(a)   an analysis of literature and other relevant documents;

(b)   three case studies for Africa, Latin America and Asia under-
      taken by outside specialists;

(c)   a contribution by technical ILO advisers working in the field,
      on training.

     This last contribution is requested from chief technical
advisers of projects within the competence of the ILO's Vocational
Training (F/PROF) and Management Development (F/MAN) branches.
It is understood that in countries where there is collaboration
between these two types of projects, a co-ordination of work is
also desirable for this contribution.

     In this way, the study in question can benefit from firsthand
information which would allow a judgement to be made on the
relationship in a given country between national training policies,
training practices of MNEs, and training activities undertaken by
the ILO.   Added to this information would be the opinions received
by the experts on possibilities of increased co-operation between
governments, projects and MNEs in the area of training;   for the
social and economic development goals of a country.

B.   Expected contributions

     Within the framework of questions asked below, the technical
advisers can themselves define the magnitude and the specific
apsects of their contributions which would be a function of their
own experience, of the special nature of the projects in the
referenced countries and of the facilities and the time at their
disposal.

The contributions can refer to one or several MNEs, reflect a particular experience or a study at the regional or national level. It would be desirable if relevant documents published by government agencies, employers' and workers' organisations or MNEs, which relate to training practices, could be sent at the earliest convenience to Geneva, in advance of the specific contribution requested by the technical advisers.

The information communicated to the ILO's Training Department (FORM) will be used in such a way that no prejudice would arise for the institution or the person from whom it was obtained. However, if the author of a contribution would not wish a country, an institute or an enterprise quoted to be identified in the study, he is requested to notify this in his report by adding a (C) after the corresponding passage. On the other hand, if he wishes an enterprise to be quoted, he should obtain the agreement of this enterprise and should naturally indicate this in his report.

As much as possible, the contributions by the technical advisers should reflect the situation found in the subsidiaries of large MNEs.

C. Framework for the contribution

    1. ILO project, MNEs and national
       training institutions

(a) It is possible that a project in view of its link with the national training institutions may make a contribution to the training of managers and technicians, administrative personnel or skilled workers in one or several MNEs operating in the country. Can you describe the characteristics, the special condition and possible difficulties of such an operation?

(b) Have the national body in question and the project under consideration, requested or benefited from assistance by one or several MNEs? Examples of such assistance may include the following: plant visits, study of training needs, detachment of trainers or lecturers, granting of fellowships, utilisation of technical facilities such as workshops, computers, machines, laboratories, reproduction facilities, etc.

(c) Has the project (with the agreement of the relevant national training body) developed one or several specific training activities, including seminars, in favour of an MNE? If yes, can you provide details?

    2. National policies and practices
       of MNEs

(a) Are there specific provisions within the framework of existing regulations aimed at the encouragement of the participation of MNEs (at all levels)? Which provisions? (For instance: tax facilities, social advantages, exemption from training tax.) Can you give your opinion on the application of these provisions?

(b) Are certain MNEs represented in governing bodies, or similar
     management boards responsible for national training policies
     or in administrative organs of institutions for the training
     of managers and technicians?   More specifically, do they
     contribute to the definition of training standards, selection
     methods, examination standards, training needs, vocational
     orientation and information, etc?

(c) Do you know of examples of voluntary contributions furnished
     by MNEs to national training efforts such as: financial and
     technical contributions; furnishing of training facilities;
     assistance for the development or creation of training insti-
     tutions, in-plant training, placement and other follow-up
     services available to trainees?

(d) Do you know of examples of training furnished directly, or
     indirectly, by MNEs in favour of other enterprises, such as
     enterprises having subcontracting relationships or using
     products or machines manufactured by an MNE?

(e) Are you in a position to appreciate the role which MNEs play
     in the brain-drain or the exodus of skilled workers?

      3. Multinational enterprises
          and training practices

(a) The decision made by an MNE to invest or expand business in
     a certain country is influenced in part by the availability
     of qualified manpower and thus by the effectiveness of the
     existing training system.   To what extent does this factor
     apply to the MNEs known by you?

(b) Can you provide information on the percentage distribution
     of professional categories, between national managers and
     technicians and expatriates, etc., in the enterprises known
     to you?   Perhaps you may wish to distinguish a third category,
     namely foreign managers and technicians locally recruited.
     What specific facilities are offered to national managers and
     technicians and foreigners locally recruited?

(c) What in-plant training and perfectioning is offered to
     national workers (volume, level, type); possibly same question
     for foreign workers locally recruited, or in respect of con-
     tracts concluded with a third country (which country?)?

(d) Indicate the means available to the MNEs (to which your report
     refers) for basic training.

(e) Do you know of MNEs furnishing a substantial programme of
     general training to their workers and their families, such as
     literacy and language training, etc.?   Can you indicate the
     features and the aims of such programmes (for instance,
     number of persons trained in this way, per year)?

(f) To the extent that it is possible to make a comparison between
     an MNE and a national enterprise of similar activity and size
     (number of workers), what are in your view the advantages and
     the disadvantages found in each of these enterprises in respect
     to the training of their personnel: facilities, obligations,
     monetary and social costs, rotation of personnel, etc.

4. <u>Personal suggestions by
   training advisers</u>

    You are certainly in a position to appreciate within the
context of the country in which you are working, or with reference
to your earlier experience, the contribution of certain MNEs to
national efforts or to the contrary, the ill-effects of such efforts
resulting from a mismatch between the practices of MNEs and the
policies applied by the national authorities. From this knowledge
you have, undoubtedly, thought about possibilities to improve the
situation. Could you furnish us with your views on this subject
for the benefit of the study?

ANNEX III

Guide for authors of case studies

Place of case studies within the global research project

The case studies will provide illustrations of in-depth analysis in various development environments of training practices of multi-national enterprises and their contribution to training efforts for development; and problems connected with this issue area. A somewhat more detailed description of the total research project is enclosed.

Type of case study

Three possibilities (or combinations of them) are open to the authors of case studies, namely: (a) a study for the country as a whole, using mainly published and other documentation, and in a complementary way, interviews; (b) a study of a region or district of a country with a concentration of implantations of multinational enterprises; and (c) a study for all units of a multinational enterprise in the country.

Given the constraints of time, resources and the usual lack of relevant published material, it is expected that authors will normally opt for a case study of type (b).[1] At the same time, extrapolations, where possible, to the situation of the country as a whole, would be desired.

Scope and organisation of case studies

On the assumptions made in the previous section, the following scope, structure and organisation is proposed to the authors:

(i)   interviews with management (general and personnel) of multinational enterprises (two or three) implanted in the region of the author's residence (usually the capital city of the country);

(ii) interviews with senior officials of the minstry responsible for training and manpower question in the national development planning context;

(iii) interviews with directors or senior staff of relevant local training institutions in the fields of vocational, technical and managerial training, co-operating with the multinational enterprises in question or seeing a need for co-operation with them;

(iv) interviews with local or national employers' associations interested in training or actually co-operating in training activities;

(v)   interviews with senior officials of union organisations represented in the enterprises in question and co-operating (where applicable), in local training efforts;

---

[1] This has indeed been the case (editor's note).

(vi) where possible, interviews with a small cross-section of workers (perhaps 10 workers in total in each enterprise covered).

No interview schedules will be established. The subjects of the interviews are to be drawn from the list of points of interest for the study attached to this guide. Thus, interviews should be unstructured and focus on the main areas of interest covered by the list of points referred to, with the necessary variations in respect to the addressees. The authors will have to judge which type of areas he can best explore with the various groups of persons and institutions with whom he will get actually in contact. In addition, points not mentioned in the list, but which the persons contacted consider important in the context of the study, should also be taken into account.

As regards the selection of multinational enterprises two to three major enterprises should be covered by the case study. If possible, enterprises working in different economic sectors and of different origin should be selected.

It is expected that authors make their own arrangements for interviews. However, should they have problems of access to respondents, they should let this be known to the ILO. The International Organisation of Employers (IOE) has promised support for the study and might be in a position to intervene where problems of access to management might arise. At any rate, the relevant ILO field offices will be informed about the project and asked to help the authors, as much as possible, with the provision of contacts or other arrangements.

If the respondents so desire, their organisations will not be identified in the study. This might in particular be true for the multinational enterprises. In any case, the names of the interviewed persons should not be identified in the reports but reference should be made to them by quoting their functions. For instance, it might be stated that "a representative of management X enterprise indicated that" or the "secretary of Y union mentioned that" or "a senior official in the Labour Ministry was of the opinion that".

In addition to the information received through interviews, the authors are expected to utilise any relevant published material and any other documents available to them or received during the interviews. Such material would, in particular, be useful as regards the part of the case study giving a brief overview of the training efforts of the country in the context of development (point (II) of the rough outline spelt out below).

Provisional outline for case studies

The proposed provisional outline is rather simple and consists of three headings as follows:

(I) Training efforts by multinational enterprises (a review of the types and volume of the various training programmes undertaken by the firms with relevance for their employees and other nationals in the country of implantation).

(II) Characteristics of national (or local) training efforts
      and systems (vocational training, technical or managerial
      training), its major priorities and functions, problem
      areas and gaps with respect to the development process.

(III) Contribution by multinational enterprises to national
      and local training efforts for development (an evaluation
      of the findings in point (I) on the background of the
      findings of point (II) above).   This evaluation is a
      specific task of the author of the case study.   It
      should, also, mention possibilities of improvements in
      the training efforts of multinational enterprises as
      felt necessary;   and priority action for a better integra-
      tion of such training efforts with the national training
      system.

Format of the case study report

     The case study should be drafted in English.   Its maximum
length should be 20-25 pages (double spaced typewritten).   Three
copies of the case study need to be sent to the ILO.   In addition
to the body of the text, relevant statistics can be appended
together with a list of source materials and of interviews undertaken.   If case notes exist on the interviews, they can be attached
if the author feels that they could provide additional information
for the concluding chapter of the general report.